I0605297

Nicolas Fouquet, portrait by Charles Le Brun, 1650

CHRISTOPHER R. SEITZ

THE PREDESTINATE

Ecclesiastes and the Man Who Outshone the Sun King

BAYLOR UNIVERSITY PRESS

Cover and book design by Elyxandra Encarnación
Cover art: Gerbrand van den Eeckhout, *Solomon's Idolatry*, c. 1665, oil on canvas. Agnes Etherington Art Centre, Queen's University, Kingston. Gift of Alfred and Isabel Bader, 2013 (56-003.15).
Frontispiece: Charles Le Brun, portrait of Nicolas Fouquet, 1650

The Library of Congress has cataloged this book under ISBN 978-1-4813-2446-5.

Library of Congress Control Number: 2025939687

Contents

Preface

The book to follow is unusual—and rich with intrigue. It will toggle between the book of Ecclesiastes and an illustrious figure of the seventeenth century, not well known outside of France. In respect of Ecclesiastes, it does not make any effort to survey in detail the individual chapters and subsections that constitute the present book. Books that do that are readily available, and, in the words of Koheleth, the making of them is endless. Instead, we prepare several overviews that capture the flow, purpose, and larger goal of this ambitious, if difficult, book.

The treatment of Ecclesiastes is, then, perspectival. In my judgment the reason people have trouble with the book and its interpretation is that they lack the proper starting point and perspective. I have the same sense about the book of Job, and for that reason just completed a small book on the topic.[1] Whose is this voice we are listening to? Why is he named Koheleth? How are we to be guided as we traverse the terrain of the twelve chapters that constitute his strange and challenging speech to us?

In what follows I will endeavor to say something about the book as a whole, and I will particularly focus on the ending and the beginning—good places from which to view a thing—but I am chiefly concerned to understand what sort

[1] *The Heights of the Hills Are His Also* (Baylor University Press, 2024).

of authorial perspective is being introduced and how we are to view the protagonist in relation to Solomon, whose name is never mentioned. I think if readers have a better sense of that, the other pieces of the puzzle of the book will begin to come into focus.

As for the man Nicolas Fouquet, you will be introduced to an extremely rare and gifted individual, whose position as Superintendent of Finances under Louis XIV gave him wealth, fame, creative talent, friends, and influence. The rapidity and severity of his fall is the stuff of legend.[2]

He is made to be the author of a volume of sayings from Solomon that, by any measurement, was a great success and achieved something like bestseller status. Because his fall comes alongside stories that likewise seek to account for Ecclesiastes by claiming it is the work of a man who, though once enormously wealthy and endowed with great wisdom, lost everything, the parallels with Fouquet are obvious.

I have said enough to give the reader some indication of the trails we will be going down. The story of Fouquet is rich in its own right, and he has been the subject of excellent biographical treatments. I have read them carefully in bringing this book to life. I will be sharing key sections of his story in light of our larger concern to gain the proper perspective on the book of Ecclesiastes.

[2] The reader will find the standard French-language treatments in the bibliography and in footnoted references to follow. English translations are my own. The treatment of Charles Drazin, *The Man Who Outshone the Sun King: Ambition, Triumph and Treachery in the Reign of Louis XIV* (Random House, 2009) provides for readers without French a very excellent account. In places where I quote him, those English translations are his own, unless I have filled in ellipses or provided wider citations from his French sources. He spells the surname of "Fouquet" in the older spelling of "Foucquet," as do a few other sources. It is the way he signed his name in the seventeenth century. Similarly, the title of the protagonist of Ecclesiastes is sometimes spelled "Koheleth" or by others "Qoheleth," a transliteration of the Hebrew. I will use the former in my remarks and will retain the latter if used in sources cited. As a final note, Scripture translations are from the RSV unless noted otherwise.

Introduction

This is a book about Ecclesiastes. It is not a commentary, and it is not another scholarly monograph. It is about how we understand the angle of vision it asks us to see if we are properly to interpret the book, its authorial perspective, and its theological and spiritual goals. The book was a sort of go-to guide down the ages on how to live our lives within proper limits, how to surrender ourselves to God, and finally how to learn to die.

Much of what I explore here centers on the matter of authorial perspective. This is because in the modern period certain views of authorship have misunderstood how divine inspiration works when it comes to biblical texts. Ecclesiastes is particularly challenging on this front. It circulates in lists and orders of the Scriptures of Israel together with Proverbs and Song of Songs, and it obviously—or so it seems—seeks to locate its wisdom in relationship to Solomon. "I was king over Israel in Jerusalem," it says, before it rehearses what are obviously meant to be (now perceived) excesses of accumulation easily related to the narratives about Solomon in the opening chapters of 1 Kings.

And yet the name of Solomon never appears, and the autobiographical reminiscences, once they are compactly registered, give way to the main burden of the book in the form of sentences or compact proverb-like statements. This is an oblique authorial referentiality, if that is not saying too much. The book is prepared to deliver its divinely inspired message without a lot of care to denotate its "author." I will have more to say about that in what follows, as it nicely comes alongside views of the book we find in the earliest history of interpretation.

My late wife and I lived about twenty minutes from what has been called "the most beautiful building in all of France," the chateau of Vaux-le-Vicomte.[1] It is the crowning achievement of Nicolas Fouquet, the one-time Superintendent of Finances under Louis XIV. This book will detail the main outlines of his story.

In a great many ways, and for our purposes, his life mirrors that of Solomon as he has been given voice in the book of Ecclesiastes. That is an observation a general student of the life of this great man could make, especially one who knows the full arc of his life and its final eighteen-year conclusion, in exile in the royal prison of Pignerol on the Italian border. His valet was, as history would have it, the enigmatic "Man in the Iron Mask."[2]

Also, as history or as Providence would have it, a volume appears shortly before what will be Fouquet's death in 1680 called *Les Conseils de la Sagesse* (1677).[3] This volume, running through numerous editions and translated into all major languages of the period, is a collection of the maxims of Solomon from sources attributed to him (including those found in Ben Sira). A paraphrase then follows, and a meditation or

[1] Charles Drazin, *The Man Who Outshone the Sun King: Ambition, Triumph and Treachery in the Reign of Louis XIV* (Random House, 2009), photo description, following p. 162.

[2] The story's grand popularization was undertaken by Alexandre Dumas in the nineteenth century: *The Man in the Iron Mask*, ed. David Coward ([1847] Oxford University Press, 1991).

[3] For full citation, see the bibliography. In our text I will speak of it as *Conseils*, *Les Conseils*, *Les Conseils de la Sagesse*, *The Counsels of Wisdom*, or *Counsels*.

reflection on its import. Significantly, it includes an introductory preface that intimates its author is none other than a Fouquet in the exile of prison. We will include the preface and key sections of *Conseils* in what follows.

There has been some considerable confusion among French historians over the true author of this collection. Some defend the Fouquet attribution, seeing the work as consistent with writings we can without doubt trace to him, composed during his prison years. Others claim the author is one Michel Boutauld S.J. We will examine the disagreement below.[4]

[4] A very good example of the running discussion is to be found in a footnote from the early nineteenth-century biographer Chatelain. He rehearses the general position of the eighteenth century, which was questioned shortly before his own work (1905) by a certain Père Sommervogel (see appendix 1 below):

> It was Vincent Placius who first attributed *Les Conseils de la Sagesse* to Foucquet in his *Treatrum anonymorum et pseudonymorum*, Hamburg, 1708, in-fol. In 1710, Christophe Myllius in the supplement to the *Theatrum* insisted on the attribution of *Les Conseils de la Sagesse* to Foucquet and relied on the authority of Berndius (*Die Christliche Sittenlehre*). J. Castre Aurigny echoed them both in the *Vies des hommes illustrés de France,* 1793, in-12, volume V. Père Sommervogel alleges that *les Conseils* appeared in 1677 and that Foucquet's papers were only brought back from Pignerol by his son, according to Cheruel, in 1683 (*L'Amie des livres*, 1862, volume IV, p. 250). But it should be noted that on the one hand, Sommervogel does not justify the attribution of this book to père Boutauld and that, on the other hand, many other writings by Foucquet left his prison before his death. The very fact that the sequel to *Les Conseils* appeared in 1683 could result from the fact that this new volume was among Foucquet's papers remaining in Pignerol. We must take more account of Berndius's admission that "Foucquet refused to recognize this work as his own." But this very protest proves that it was attributed to him during his lifetime. Père Sommervogel does a better job of establishing that *Le Theologien dans les conversations avec les sages et les grands du monde* is to be reinstated to père Coton. (Urbain-Victor Chatelain, *Le Surintendant Nicolas Foucquet, protecteur des lettres des arts et des sciences* [Perrin, 1905], 546–47)

This is the French and German discussion. In chapter 3 below we examine the English translation of 1734 where the Fouquet attribution is likewise assumed, and indeed it is the strong entry point for the translator's composition.

In either case, however, we have a very good picture of the penitent Fouquet in prison and the writings he produced during this period. The proximity in thought to Ecclesiastes makes a matter of intrigue (and also of some indifference) whether *Les Conseils* comes from his hand or not. Clearly someone wanted to give this impression, as the preface shows, and the general public certainly believed the work to be his. As we shall see, this view of the authorship of a very popular work persisted.

Comparing the situation of *Les Conseils* with Ecclesiastes on the matter of authorship and how we evaluate it as a category important for the text's interpretation, we may put forward this consideration. The content of the writings produced by Fouquet at Pignerol and the content of the meditations in *Conseils* (as well as the selections chosen from Ecclesiastes, Proverbs, and Ben Sira) are in significant ways overlapping. Indeed, one of the major English translations (whose translator understands the work to be that of Fouquet) points to meditations he judges perfectly suited to Fouquet's situation in prison. One finds what one is looking for, one might surmise. We examine this work in detail below.

But the interesting point to be noted, I believe, is how this generic congruence (it is maximal in the preface itself) relativizes authorship as a determinative category for interpretation. If someone wanted to create the impression that Fouquet was the author, it was not difficult to do. His fate in prison was common knowledge, and this would persist in Paris throughout his long confinement. He and the Solomon being referred to and taken as a source of wise counsel share similar circumstances, and that is true not just in the selections made from Ecclesiastes in particular but also those maxims chosen from Proverbs and Ben Sira. They share a landscape of penitential confession and surrender to God's purposes. Their common link is scriptural and "Solomonic."

This all comes alongside the final writings of Nicolas Fouquet as they have been preserved to us.[5] His place of scriptural preference, wherein he understands his situation and his proper obedience to God as King, is the Psalms of David. The common terrain of spiritual insight in all these cases is an inscripted one.

We believe that one hindrance to a proper understanding of the book of Ecclesiastes is a certain preoccupation with what I would call a thin account of "authorship." And, as well, of historical reference. The book has been made to exist primarily in accounts of its authorship and the historical circumstances of its composition according to modern critical theories about that, which are, as with all such things, not of one mind. This prevents us from gaining the proper perspective on how the book has sought to situate itself vis-à-vis Solomon, in a unique portrayal that is different in kind than claims to his authoring the work before us. The "author" of *Les Conseils* has likewise "given voice" to the imprisoned and penitent Fouquet, however we might understand claims to authorship in relation to that work. We are fortunate to have historical records from after his life, which confirm the "fit." This is simply a mystery of Providence, as one might say.

In this book we want to keep Fouquet and the Ecclesiast on the same common terrain. The story of the former is rich, profound, moving; it is a true story about a flesh-and-blood man who spent his last eighteen years in prison, sixteen of them in alpine exile from family and friends and from a life of accomplishment and generosity—whatever may have been his imprudent misdemeanors on the canvas of the seventeenth century and an age of wealth and patronage.

The story holds its own intrigue, populated with characters like The Man in the Iron Mask and the head of the Three Musketeers, d'Artagnan, who would become his close friend.

[5] We are fortunate in having long portions of these texts, in a variety of genres, available in the several Fouquet bibliographies of the recent period.

Solomon's story, when one reads through the first ten chapters of 1 Kings, appears in many ways no less exotic and also truly *sans pareil.* Any modern reader pauses and says, "Can that indeed be true?" Then chapter 11 arrives and a very different Solomon is brought to our attention.

But the thing they most truly share, and which Ecclesiastes seeks to show us—as *Les Conseils* does in its way—are men broken and penitent and, just to the degree that is so, coming to their spiritual senses.

1
The Predestinate

It was a warm Sunday afternoon in fall, one of the very best times to be in Paris. After Mass at St Ignace in the 7th arrondissement, I decided walking would be the best way to get to my destination. I wanted to visit the historic Chapel of the Sisters of the Visitation in the Marais, just short of the Place des Vosges.[1] After the Revolution the church was sold to the Protestant Église Reformée Unie, and I was assuming worship would already be over for the day. And yet, although a historical monument (the sign greeted me as I arrived) it was now an active parish church. I noted that during the week the opening hours were fairly limited, and that I would be busy with other affairs. And, as stated, it was a nice day for a long walk.

I opened the door and was a bit surprised as a service was underway. The church still had all the feel of a seventeenth-century Catholic edifice, but oddly enough the service underway was in Arabic, or so I would learn. I was not there for that purpose and quietly told the team at the rear what I was seeking. "Could you tell me the way to the crypt where Nicolas

[1] The historical church is known by a variety of names: "Saint Marie of the Angels," "The Daughters of the Visitation," the chapel of "The Convent of the Visitation to Saint Mary." The historical marker reads, "Ancienne église du couvent des filles de la Visitation Sainte-Marie," since it is presently "Temple Protestant du Marais."

Fouquet is buried?" Biographies of this man all indicate that, after his long imprisonment in the royal fortress of Pignerol on the Italian border and his death there in 1680, one year later his body was transferred to this very place.

"Who is Nicolas Fouquet?" a friendly voice responded in hushed tones. Realizing this was probably a question other colleagues there might better answer, I was handed on to a very welcoming young man. I assumed I was dealing with the worship team or church leadership of some kind, and I explained in French that I was a Christian, a pastor, doing research. It was he who explained that this was a service for an Arabic-speaking congregation, and that indeed a bit later a Japanese congregation would arrive. Intrigued with this for its own sake, I nevertheless pressed on.

"Do you know that this was the chapel of a religious order associated with good works and care for the poor and sick, and that Mme Fouquet [whose son's grave I was in search of] was associated with its founding?" No, he did not. "This a Protestant church," he said flatly.

Unaware of the significance of this history or of the man Nicolas Fouquet—the richest man in France and the Superintendent of Finances under none other than Louis XIV—and his final resting place here, he had to be assured that I wasn't making any of this up. I did wonder with some puzzlement how these friendly people were so completely unaware of the historical origins of their church and indeed of this extremely important man, a sort of Rothschild, Thomas Jefferson, and John Paul Getty all rolled into one.

I was led to believe that there was no crypt or that, minimally, one could not view something they had no knowledge of. Leaving, I paused to examine the historical monument plaque once again and noted that, while it spoke of the origins of the seventeenth-century Couvent des filles de la Visitation, there was indeed no reference to the Fouquet tomb. That much they seemed to have got right.

But why no mention, given that he is indeed buried here?

The fate of Nicolas Fouquet is ironically tied up with a man to whom the passage of time would give far more attention—even as we know nothing of him *as part of what makes him who he is*, which has given scope for vast speculation, that is, as the Man in the Iron Mask.

The man whose name and accomplishments were once as widely recognized as the younger famed Sun King whom he served effectively lost his name. His grave, like that of Moses, unmarked.

Then we have the masked man, the stuff of endless intrigue and raucous fictionalization to the point of surfeit: Three Musketeers, d'Artagnan, Count of Monte Cristo, Alexandre Dumas's celebrated bringing-to-life and filling-in-the-blanks, nineteenth-century accomplishment. A movie with Leonardo di Caprio (in—spoiler alert—two roles!). On it goes. American Halloween costumes, flashing rapiers at the ready. Darth Vader taking over where this Iron Mask left off.

This only underscores the irony. A Great Man with a name loses his name and is lost to history. The man without a name—and likely a mere valet, the man who served our man Fouquet in Pignerol in his last years—theatrically overfilling history.[2]

[2] Daniel Dessert concludes his superb biography *Fouquet* in this way, in comparing the legacy of Fouquet to that of his successor Jean-Baptiste Colbert, who saw to his ruin.

> Fouquet will therefore never know the posthumous glory which praises 'The Great Man.' He was ignominiously chased from History by the fury of wicked men. He only survives through an architectural marvel, born of a fatal passion and distinguished taste. He paid the highest price for his faults, but Heaven granted him grace in compensation. He did not have, like his rival at Saint-Eustache, the kind of destiny which inevitably leads to a vain cenotaph. He rests in peace, forgotten and anonymous. In the end, however, it is far from clear that Nicolas had the lesser part. (*Fouquet* [Fayard, 1987], 343)

The rival referred to is Jean-Baptiste Colbert.

Biographies tell us that Fouquet's mother requested his body be brought back and buried here—the son she had prayed for tirelessly. That done, she died one month later. A woman of extreme Christian virtue and humble service.[3]

Fouquet was sixty-five when the conditions of his exile exhausted him, still believing he would soon be released after eighteen years of captivity by an increasingly lenient Louis XIV, now in his forties. He died in the arms of his son who had been permitted to visit.

Fouquet's casket is indeed here, in the family crypt, be it unnamed.

The death notes will read thus, recorded by the Sisters of the Visitation who received his body into the Fouquet family crypt.

> On 28 March 1681, Monsieur Nicolas Foucquet was buried in our church, in the chapel of Saint Francis de Sales . . . In the great offices he held, he demonstrated so extraordinary a talent, so noble a manner and such just and generous feeling, that the past centuries can offer almost no one to rival his accomplishments. But God, who wanted to make a Predestinate, overturned all these great earthly achievements. He was disgraced, in spite of his important services, put on trial and imprisoned for more than eighteen years. It was during this trial that, stripped of all his honours, he rediscovered virtue and experienced the enlightenment of faith. He began to open his eyes and to recognize the emptiness of worldly splendours . . . So it was that by his disgrace he changed his ways, achieved sanctity and died, full of good deeds and righteousness before God.[4]

[3] For a sample, see appendix 3.

[4] Reproduced in Charles Drazin, *The Man Who Outshone the Sun King: Ambition, Triumph and Treachery in the Reign of Louis XIV* (Random House, 2009), 303–4. I provide the full version below.

In this book we are endeavoring to understand the way the author of Ecclesiastes has given voice to a penitent Solomon likewise brought to his knees. As early Jewish and then Christian sources would say, noting the book does not name his name, this is the King who burned incense to other gods and lost his previously rich and sumptuous way. His royal signet ring was taken from him as was his name. He wandered in penitence and said, "I am Koheleth."[5]

We judge the protagonist of the book of Ecclesiastes as someone akin to "the man who outshone the Sun King"; who in the end found his way back to God; and who before his death came to understand the difference between earthly achievements and the True King. That Solomon was himself a king (and for the bulk of the scriptural testimony an exemplary one) makes the story to be here related all the more relevant and compelling.

Like Fouquet's, Solomon's renown went out, in the idiom of the book of Kings, to the proverbial "ends of the world." Like Fouquet's, his fame included gardens and fine buildings exceeding all others in beauty and refinement, the accumulation of goods and riches, ships, chariots, horses, and collections of wise sayings and other emblems of great learning. Fouquet was not a king, yet about him Voltaire would write in the following decades:

> On 17 August, at six in the evening Fouquet was the King of France: at two in the morning, he was a nobody.[6]

Such was the extent of his fame. The family motto of the Fouquet's was "Where will he not ascend?" and in time became "How far will he be asked to descend?"

The Fouquet story is a real one, chronicled by real historians and biographers. We are fortunate in having a clear record

[5] The full text is found below in chapter 7.

[6] "Le 17 août, à six heures du soir, Fouquet était roi du France; à deux heures du matin, il n'était pas rien" (Voltaire, *Le Siècle de Louis XIV* [Berlin, 1751]).

of the time he was forced to spend in the prison that would be his final home, how he conducted himself, and what he would in time be free to write down for us to read. It is a story of confession, of abject descent, and eventually of spiritual peace and insight.

What makes the story even more interesting—this for itself and also for the proper interpretation of the book of Ecclesiastes—is a volume that would appear in the final years of his imprisonment titled *Les Conseils de la Sagesse* (1677). The volume is anonymous. It is a nearly five-hundred-page collection of the sentences and sayings of Solomon, with a paraphrase for those selected and a meditation to follow. These are taken from Proverbs, Ecclesiastes, Song of Songs, and Ben Sira. The volume was widely circulated, went through several editions, and was translated into every major language of the day. The subtitle reads: "A Collection of Such Maxims of Solomon as are Most Necessary for the prudent Conduct of Life: With Proper Reflections upon Them."

We have English translations of this popular volume being made well into the following century. These are interesting for the opening commendations the translators typically include and what they say about the book's earliest reception history, given that the work is anonymous, on the one hand, and is itself a compendium of scriptural maxims traditionally thought to be the work of King Solomon, on the other (this being so, as well, with the manifestly later Ben Sira, which at best would amount to a supplement to what we would otherwise expect to be attributed to the successor of King David).

The 1677 French edition begins with a short preface. The "author" describes the conditions of his writing and the state of his mind, before the maxims appear with paraphrase and reflections. He is in a place of solitude, and the immediate reaction one would naturally have is that we are hearing about none other than Nicolas Fouquet in exile in Pignerol. This linkage is taken for granted in the translations just mentioned, and it is key to how the various commendations seek to make their point. "O wise person, Lord, noble, etc., learn from Monsieur Nicolas Fouquet." We will have more to say about this.

The 1677 volume, whoever one might conjecture wrote it, finds us some thirteen years into the very publicly known imprisonment of Fouquet in Pignerol, so the association of the volume with him—leaving aside for a moment the motivation for writing the preface—would be immediately logical. Who else could it be?

It is important to note that there is a difference between what we can know about Fouquet, given subsequent historiographical research and documents that fill out the picture of this illustrious man's imprisonment, and what the author of the preface could know in the mid-seventies of the seventeenth century. The entire point of royal imprisonment via so-called *lettres de cachet* is to make said prisoner disappear. We know from our different vantage point far more than what someone publishing *Les Conseils* with its preface could know. And this includes a considerable correspondence running back and forth from Louis XIV's Minister of War, and indeed the king himself, and the (important for the time) head jailor, Benigné Dauvergne de Saint-Mars, concerning Fouquet and the conditions of his life in prison in remote Pignerol.

In time the author of *Les Conseils* will be identified as a certain Michel Boutauld, a Parisian Jesuit whose dates makes him ten years older than Fouquet. How that identification comes to be made is something of a mystery. We know very little about him. Fouquet was educated amongst Jesuits in Paris, and his mother, as we have noted, was a woman devoted to the Catholic faith, eight out of nine of her children entering religious life.[7] More of a mystery, if that were possible, is what motivated him to attribute the work to Fouquet, which the preface most certainly did.

Fouquet would die three years after the appearance in Paris of *Les Conseils*, but of course the author could know less of

[7] See appendix 3 below.

that than of the concrete conditions of his exile, which he is therefore forced only to intimate in generalized terms, much as any sympathetic author at a distance might do.

What interests me for the purpose of the present work is what it might mean to "give voice" to someone, which in the case of Nicolas Fouquet—who will indeed die in March of 1680—ends up being something like his personal legacy, his last will and testament, the words of a man chastened in the same manner as he who said, "Vanity of vanities, all is vanity," before being made to offer his own final testament in the final chapter of Ecclesiastes. That is, to give voice to a Nicolas Fouquet, who will repeat that verse refrain from the corpus associated in the seventeenth century with King Solomon, paraphrase and comment on it, and do so likewise in the massively influential and widely read volume attributed to him.

We can better appreciate a thing by finding something similar to it and then comparing and contrasting. I am interested in appreciating the achievement of the book of Ecclesiastes, what in ancient hermeneutics was called its *dianoia*—its larger purpose, appreciated best when one understands the structure, shape, and force of the whole. Solomon is not named in a book that means to evoke him. Why is that? Fouquet is not mentioned in a book that means to invoke him. Why is that?

One of the terms of imprisonment that Saint-Mars was instructed to strictly enforce was to forbid Fouquet from writing of any kind. For a man whose entire life was in the domain of letters, this was particularly harsh. He wrote on his clothes, tablecloths, pieces of ribbon, rags—but in time even that was disallowed. His laundry regime was tightly monitored. He was trying to maintain any semblance of normalcy or continuation of a prior life. The point of Pignerol was to silence and to make disappear. When Dumas popularized the idea of the "Man in the Iron Mask" in the nineteenth century, one thing he was saying—apart from the accuracy of what he was reporting—was that the absolute monarchy of Louis XIV was not above soldering an iron mask onto a human head so that the identity of said person could not be known.

In time, and for reasons not entirely conclusive, these restrictions were lifted.[8] On one occasion, having caught some news about financial straits—again, he was not permitted any news of affairs outside his exile—Fouquet offered to write to the king and proffer what had previously been invaluable advice. Paper and pen were brought. All of this was closely monitored. His advice, he would learn, was of no interest; the return correspondence was read aloud to him and then burned in his presence for effect.

Louis XIV would then ease matters considerably and allow him to write his wife and his mother, and to write more generally. This is how we can know about his penitent frame of mind (more on that below). The contents of these letters are revealing and moving, particularly in the case of writing to his mother. He had burdened his mother through his refusal to heed her and his chaplain's warnings about his excessive accumulation of goods—books, art, ancient manuscripts—and his obviously lax Catholic life of prayer and devotion. That his better in this was Cardinal Mazarin himself mattered little to them. He had been raised in a devout family and educated among Jesuits. They worried about the man who would one day imprudently "outshine the Sun King."

I cited the death notice above. Some have conjectured that his mother (and perhaps his sisters) helped with its composition. This rings true in the sense that she knew about his contrition and new manner of life and frame of mind in prison from the

[8] Louvois, the Secretary of War, was charged with high-priority prisoners like Fouquet. He wrote the Royal Jailor Saint-Mars on behalf of Louis XIV; the correspondence is considerable. Later on (1678), rather than making his response to Saint-Mars, who would in turn convey it, Louvois will allow Fouquet to write him directly. Further, as he was suffering from eye problems, and because Fouquet had observed his mother's many successful medicinal treatments, he became the beneficiary of his medical assistance, which greatly relieved his ailment. They would become more than cordial and indeed developed a genuine friendship (on this see Dessert, *Fouquet*, 282).

letters she had received from him. The jailor Saint-Mars would likewise comment on the peaceful composure and religious devotion of Fouquet, especially in what would be his later years in Pignerol. He had been given greater access to the confessional, and the Mass schedule was increased. He paid close attention to his daily devotions and observance of feast days. His reading material was entirely religious and devotional in character.

The word used to characterize him in this notice is not one we customarily hear in a nominal form, "Predestinate." Biblical texts like Ephesians 1:11–12 may come to mind: "In him we were also chosen, having been predestined according to the plan of him who works out everything in conformity with the purpose of his will" (NIV). The term apparently arises in the fifteenth century, likely based on scriptural texts like this, in reference to a person "foreordained to an earthly or eternal lot or destiny by divine decree." While within the limited scope of those who took care for his body and his final resting place, or who knew what his mother was given to know about her son's latter days, that makes a certain amount of sense. And so the text reads, "But God, who wanted to make a Predestinate."

At the time of his internment, and given the conditions of his body being placed in an unmarked grave, we might wonder, Who but God—and some close friends and relatives—would understand this once grand man of affairs as "foreordained to an earthly or eternal lot or destiny by divine decree"? The historiography of our era allows us to piece together an account that would permit us to draw a conclusion like this, should we be so inclined. The unknown Man in the Iron Mask has, however, outshone the man who outshone the Sun King, if we let history go its way and tell its story.

Les Conseils de la Sagesse, we might rightly conclude, did in fact give to history a man "Predestinate" and allow his "voice" to arise. The further fascination entails the gap referred to above, namely, that we can now know what Fouquet's spiritual state of mind was, thanks to archives and documentation, in ways the brief preface intimating him could only guess at and sketch out in modest form. And what we find is that gap is in fact closing. The author of *Conseils*, using the vehicle of a sober, wise, and clear-thinking Solomon, captures for us the man Fouquet and bequeaths that portrait to generations anxious to open the book in translation and learn properly how to conduct oneself in this life "under the sun," as the subtitle states it.

And what of King Solomon himself, whose last days as recorded in the book of Kings cast a considerably dark shadow over whatever we might deem his great achievements, to the point of canceling them out? Is this the last word? His grave is not unmarked, but what of his legacy, and how shall this man be properly evaluated, leaving aside the typical terse refrains of the historian editing what is called the Deuteronomistic History? How shall we speak of him, and what shall history say?

It is the judgment of this present study that the book of Ecclesiastes represents something of the same achievement vis-à-vis Solomon that *Les Conseils* brings to fruition for the Superintendent of Finances, the "royal" man who stabilized France after the Fronde, gave a kingdom to Louis XIV saved from financial ruin, and in his turn built the "most beautiful house in France," the chateau of Vaux-le-Vicomte south of Paris.

My aim here is not to burden the reader with another biography of Fouquet. Very good ones are ready to hand. We will rather focus on those key moments in his life and those significant literary remains that help us understand how the family motto, "To where will he not ascend?" will prove right in the end.

And what we seek to know about the Superintendent of Finances in respect of his public legacy, given the length of his life and his final destiny, we seek to know about the equally famous Solomon depicted in the book of Ecclesiastes, whose final fate is set before us in this, his last will and testament.

2

The Preacher Says Goodbye

The Voice from the End of Life

I can recall preparing introductory lectures for the basic Old Testament survey course in my first post. Though I had been trained by the esteemed Sterling Professor at Yale, Brevard Childs, I was only minimally acquainted with the work that best indicated the direction of his future thinking, *Introduction to the Old Testament as Scripture* (1979). I needed a textbook for seminarians, and his served the purpose of at least focusing on the final form and full contents of each biblical book. Surely that was what any good survey of the Old Testament for first-year students needed.

When I came to his treatment on Ecclesiastes, I was surprised. I and my fellow graduate students were well aware of the usual treatment of this book, as it would appear in then-popular introductions to "wisdom literature," the term of use popularized in the nineteenth and twentieth centuries. Ecclesiastes was a book of pessimism, resignation, futility—"carpe diem" being its only minimally uplifting leitmotif. This belongs to the idea of there being a "wisdom literature" classification itself (something the orders of Old Testament books do not state in these terms). I will have more to say about this in a later chapter, but the basic idea is that the conservative and positive appraisal of wisdom found in Proverbs gives way at the end in its rejection by Koheleth, along with the God thought to have been its source. Job stands in the middle of this journey, and that book's editorial history bears witness to a certain equivocation on the status of wisdom as useful for life and as reliably given by God.

Childs, whose work in the history of interpretation was significant, offered in passing a comment on how Ecclesiastes was heard in previous generations. Far from being a book on a journey to pessimism and futility, it was widely held to be one of the most significant, and central, of all the books in the Old Testament library. Its message was of a higher character, as it dealt with life and death and how to conduct oneself in the face of especially the latter. It was not at odds with Proverbs—another of the three Solomonic works, including Song of Songs—but was complementary to it, if operating on what one might call a more ambitious plane. In a chapter to follow I will revisit the canonical logic inhabiting the idea of a triad of Solomonic works and how this influences their respective interpretation.

A canonical reading of Ecclesiastes will pay special attention to the opening and concluding sections of the book, for that is where we are given some sense of the larger "mind" (*dianoia*) we are meant to be appreciating as we traverse the terrain of this twelve-chapter work. A reading that highlights futility and absurdity does so in part because it takes the sentences (terse sayings akin to proverbs, but now bent in a different direction) as the chief lens of interpretation. "Things that are bent cannot be straightened" is either a statement of resignation before a "bent" world, or it belongs inside of a journey the author is asking us to take in order to understand the larger mind of the whole book.

In truth, there are indeed bent and crooked things in the created order that cannot be made straight without first breaking them. Think of a tree branch. Whether that is a morally evil thing or a morally neutral or even morally generative thing is another matter, requiring us to grasp the totality of the present work in order to evaluate what individual sentences may mean inside this larger whole. Incidentally, it is also to be observed that the sentences of the first half of the work are themselves of a different character than those of the second half. This imparts to the book a certain loose narrativity, which provides some minimal structure for considering what is otherwise a diverse assembly of sayings, punctuated by the positive commendations that overlay both halves. All of this belongs within the realm of appreciating the book's *dianoia* and final interpretive purpose.

The end of a work can show us the trajectory of the work and the terrain toward which it is finally heading. This is all the more true when the conclusion is unique and particularized, as is surely the case with chapter 12 of Ecclesiastes, measured against what proceeds. It can belong nowhere in this book except where it now is. Its sense would be voided, and it would only confuse and befuddle. Ecclesiastes offers sufficient interpretive challenges as it now exists, without further complicating things. We are asked to listen to the Preacher's last words. His words on his deathbed, as it were.

The source of what follows is a talk given to a seminary audience in morning chapel. I was asked to supply a title, and I offered "The Preacher Says Goodbye." To anticipate, in the next chapter I will return to Nicolas Fouquet and what we can know about the circumstances of (what would be) his last days on earth, and especially his frame of mind and spiritual bearings. Imprisoned, but in some ways also more liberated than ever over the long course of his illustrious life and downfall.

A publication commendation on the back of *The Man Who Outshone the Sun King* reads: "From a glittering zenith as King Louis XIV's finance minister, builder of the breathtaking chateau of Vaux-le-Vicomte, collector of books, patron of the arts and lover of beautiful women, Fouquet had fallen like Icarus. Charged with embezzlement and treachery he was convicted and sentenced to life imprisonment." We will learn what that imprisonment would finally come to mean, in terms of a profound spiritual transformation like, but also distinctive from, what the book of Ecclesiastes offers in giving voice to a Solomon likewise transformed.

The Preacher Says Goodbye: Ecclesiastes 12:1–14

12 Remember also your Creator in the days of your youth,
before the evil days come, and the years draw nigh, when
you will say, "I have no pleasure in them"; [2] before the
sun and the light and the moon and the stars are darkened
and the clouds return after the rain; [3] in the day when
the keepers of the house tremble, and the strong men are
bent, and the grinders cease because they are few, and
those that look through the windows are dimmed, [4] and
the doors on the street are shut; when the sound of the
grinding is low, and one rises up at the voice of a bird,
and all the daughters of song are brought low; [5] they are
afraid also of what is high, and terrors are in the way; the
almond tree blossoms, the grasshopper drags itself along
and desire fails; because man goes to his eternal home,
and the mourners go about the streets; [6] before the silver
cord is snapped, or the golden bowl is broken, or the
pitcher is broken at the fountain, or the wheel broken at
the cistern, [7] and the dust returns to the earth as it was,
and the spirit returns to God who gave it. [8] "Vanity of
vanities," says the Preacher; "all is vanity."

[9] Besides being wise, the Preacher also taught the
people knowledge, weighing and studying and arranging
proverbs with great care. [10] The Preacher sought to find
pleasing words, and uprightly he wrote words of truth.

[11] The sayings of the wise are like goads, and like nails
firmly fixed are the collected sayings which are given
by one Shepherd. [12] My son, beware of anything beyond
these. Of making many books there is no end, and much
study is a weariness of the flesh.

[13] The end of the matter; all has been heard. Fear God,
and keep his commandments; for this is the whole duty

of man. [14] For God will bring every deed into judgment, with every secret thing, whether good or evil.

My Old Testament colleague at Yale, Robert Wilson, is known for his wry sense of humor. He hails from the state of Mitch McConnell. They have something of the same dry manner. At the bottom of the exam paper he would prepare for introductory courses, he placed a quote from Psalm 50:9 in bold font: "**I will accept no bull from your house**."

One clever student wrote in a response with a line from our text for today. "Much study is a weariness of the flesh."

We've just heard the final words from Koheleth. Words he has struggled to find. His last act is to lift his eyes from his struggle to speak to us. Words of admonition. Words to caution us. "My son, beware of anything beyond these."

One of my favorite books, *The Blue Boy*, is an autobiography written by the French author Jean Giono.[1] In it he recalls the last words of his aging father, before he headed off to the Great War. 1.4 million dead. His father was a cobbler. He lived deep down in life. Caring for the outcast and broken of the world, full of life, but cautious about its pitfalls.

He is reminiscing with his son about a subscription to a journal he had taken out. The central panel of each issue was the reproduction of a famous painting, meant to be removed and posted on a familiar wall. "The Arm of Steel." "The Mysteries of Paris." "The Wandering Jew." Well-known themes. One might well imagine, "The Man in the Iron Mask."

An issue arrived one day, and the painting was "The Fall of Icarus." You may remember the Greek legend. Icarus's father Daedalus concocts a special wax, allowing him to glue feathers to his arms so that he can fly. Then his son Icarus receives his own wings. With a Koheleth-like warning: Enjoy the flying, but do not go too high. Icarus does just that, the wax melts, and he falls to his death.

[1] Jean Giono, *Jean le Bleu* (Éditions Bernard Grasset, 1932); English translation, *Blue Boy*, Katherine A. Clark (Viking Press, 1946).

What puzzled Giono's father was that, though the painting bore this title, the canvas didn't seem to be reproducing it. It showed instead a grand scene, an effort to include the whole world, busy at day-to-day activities. Fishing, plowing, eating, brawling, giving birth. Here is a line toward the end of his description. The cadences remind me of the seven-verse sentence in our text today.

> The fields were teeming with work. Men were plowing, others sowing, harvesting, gathering in the grapes, threshing the grain, winnowing, kneading the dough, dragging the oxen forward, beating the donkey, reining in the horse, raising the hoe, the ax, the pick, or pressing so hard against the plow that their hooves dug into the furrows.

The cobbler said to himself, "They have the wrong title, the Fall of Icarus."

"That evening I lit my lamp, and there it was. High above that teeming life, all that was carrying on, unmindful. A speck in the sky. Burned to a cinder the size of the tip of my finger. Icarus was falling. Remember that, my son."

The end of Ecclesiastes sounds a similar note.

The father knew he had a son who would fly high, become the famous author he did become, and threaten to lose sight of what mattered in life. The rhythms given to us by God to live within.

I am focusing on the last lines of Ecclesiastes because that is the destination toward which the book is driving. Wisdom, we learn there, is about seeing life on its true, proper scale, just as with the painting of the Fall of Icarus. Living within God's good and rich creation on the dimensions he has provided for it. God's rich world, not the high-flying speck.

Solomon scaled great heights. Collected great things. Accomplished all that his or any heart might desire. Soared into heaven, scorched by his own grand making.

It is a very simple thing to conclude that unhappiness, physical stress or misery, restlessness, heartache could be resolved by just the right potions of pleasure, health, knowledge, or profit, and that the something missing is something we should be able to work hard at to correct. Solomon is an example of success on just that kind of logic. We follow him to the heights and see the wax melt.

He has to learn how to see things with true wisdom.

I toggle between calling the hero of the book Solomon and also Koheleth. The Preacher. That is because the book itself intends this. We are to have Solomon in view, but also Everyman. The old Adam into whose nostrils God breathed life. You and me alongside the king. We would misread the book if we thought of it as too singularly focused on a wealthy king. "That's not me or my problem." No, the book wants to speak to the acquisitional in us all.

The heart of the text we have just heard is unlike any passage in Scripture. In form and content, it is not a sentence but rather something like waves lapping against a shore. Produced by a rock thrown into the pond of life. Soon to slow and cease and be still forever. A shimmering surface that lives on after us. As the spirit leaves the body. The mirror placed before the dying mouth, which fogs no more.

One does not need to have Hebrew to catch the effect. The words are clear enough. But what do they mean, or do they mean several things at once?

The keepers of the house: our skeletal frame. The bent back of old age. The grinders—our last good teeth—now only a few are left. Early rising, as the old need less sleep. The loss of hearing that makes sharp noises startling. Fear of heights as we descend the stairs, groggy in the morning.

Yet they are also real images of the life outside of us. Mourners at our funeral. The breaking and shattering of precious things. The wheel that conveyed us, broken at the well of life. As one scholar has commented: It is as if the world is ceasing—our own.[2] That the word *hebel* at ground

[2] Michael V. Fox, "Aging and Death in Qoheleth 12," *JSOT* 42 (1988): 55–77; see also his *Ecclesiastes: The Traditional Hebrew Text with the New JPS Translation*, JPS Bible Commentary (Jewish Publication Society, 2004).

level means something to do with breath is surely significant. The breath shunted into our lungs when we cry out at birth, returning to our creator who gave it. *Hebel hebelim*, says the Preacher, one final time.

On a personal note, my marathon-"acquisitional" wife was diagnosed with a rare lung ailment and went on a five-year journey of daily decline. At the end, the breath that gives life could barely lap against a shore, brought to her now by respiratory machines working at full throttle. The snares of death entangled her. So I know something of the force of these last words from our hero. As does everyone who has closed the eyes of a loved one at death. In her case, rescued by a lung transplant at a Paris hospital with days to live.

It is in this spirit I want us to consider Koheleth. The Acquisition Man. Mr Accumulator. Mr Had It All. And finally, Mr Can't Take It With You. He will go through a painful detox. DTs and fright. Disorientation and confoundedness. From confident-if-pained declarations to questions and surrender. We can learn much from his words at the end.

But his real gift to us is his life. His confession. His acknowledgment that wisdom and possessions do not increase mathematically. They must arrive in our hands as gifts. For the one who says, "I have made many books," one must hear back, "No, you were given them, were blessed to speak them forth. They are not yours and never were. To the degree they have value, they are for the ages."

The church fathers thought of Koheleth as the Christ who descended to the depths of our lived, vain existence, plumbing it fully in all of its vanity, sharing its darkest points where no light shines, down to the depths of death itself.[3] And then by his risen life lifting Koheleth, and those he has come to claim, setting them free for service that will cost everything. So as to gain a joy the world cannot give under the sun.

[3] See the final section of Jennie Barbour, *The Story of Israel in the Book of Qoheleth: Ecclesiastes as Cultural Memory* (Oxford University Press, 2012).

Not an Icarus-like fall to death, but a fall into the sea called baptism, where we die and rise with new life altogether. Following the Christ who gives men and women the power to live with limitation, mystery, not always knowing, the hardships and adversities that are a part of the journey of life. Making them enriching after all, because of him and his victory in which we march.

The final chapter of Ecclesiastes lets the Preacher, the man, the "single brooding consciousness" we have been following through this book, finally say goodbye. It belongs to the destiny of every man one day to say goodbye, and to learn how to prepare for that last day and last moment.

To help understand the force of this last chapter and its purpose on the canvas of life, we want now to turn to another man who fell like Icarus. And whose imprisonment in Pignerol would come to mean something like his actual, eternal liberation.

3
The Superintendent Says Goodbye
The Voice from Exile

The basic facts of the life of Nicolas Fouquet are well known. He has been the subject of several very good historical treatments. Usually, people speak of the fateful dinner he hosted for Louis XIV as the occasion of his downfall. That has a nice economy and theatricality. The chateau of Vaux-le-Vicomte and the evening of August 17 merely put the flame to the fuse on an already smoldering pile of tinder. Louis XIV, along with Jean-Baptiste Colbert (who would be Fouquet's replacement), had been plotting against Fouquet for some time.

The Sun King arrives from the grand royal estate just south at Fontainebleau for a lavish dinner and attendant festivities, fireworks, a play by Molière, and the simple drinking in of Fouquet's grand achievement, the chateau of Vaux-le-Vicomte. Considering his gold-plate settings and the sheer magnificence of the "most beautiful house in all of France," this is something of the "nail in the coffin" in his decision to denounce and place on trial the finance minister. He refuses to spend the night in the special rooms being prepared for him. Even today, when you visit and come to these rooms, you will see how the painted ceilings by the celebrated Le Brun just trail off. The funds were cut off immediately upon Louis XIV's departure. The grand project of Vaux would grind to a halt. The master craftsmen whom Fouquet had assembled would now find new assignments at what would be the palace of Versailles.

Fouquet was not just Superintendent of Finances; he also held a position with the Parlement that gave him immunity from prosecution. He had earned both of these important roles by the skill with which he kept France in good budgetary shape, and he had built up a huge network of financiers and other high-level retainers. Arguably, he was the best-connected man in France. He had bought the Island of Belle Île and fortified it. Prior to the magnificent building project at Vaux, the chateau residence of Saint Mandé in the eastern suburbs of Paris was filled to the brim with ancient manuscripts, rare books, and art from Italy. He was on good terms with the royal family, the mother of Louis XIV in particular, and in the charmed company of Richelieu and then Mazarin he held on to considerable levers of power. He was not just an advisor, friend, confidant to Cardinal Mazarin, but also held his fate in his hands when the Parlement banished the unpopular Italian prelate.

Again, a thumbnail is all that is necessary to give the context for his downfall and the sheer height from which that dramatic fact would unfold. The legal process would take three years; during this time he was also under guard, exiled from Paris in various prisons. (The head of the Three Musketeers, Charles de Batz de Castlemore d'Artagnan, was his personal guard and, in time, close friend). His life as he had come to know it was over. And no one was more surprised than he. He had given everything he had to the young king he served, and perhaps the hardest blow was the discovery that it was the king himself who was charging him with financial impropriety as well as lèse-majesté. The plot to have this arrive on his doorstep was in the works for some time and long before he was aware of it. It is hard to imagine the shock that came upon him.

Another way to put it, returning to the fateful evening at the chateau of Vaux-le-Vicomte: No one embezzling funds in complex, illegal, and conniving fashion would be so imprudent as to invite the young king, coming into his powers, to come and share with him this stunning achievement. Fouquet was a man of his age, and an extremely successful one. Patronage and reward was the air being breathed in the seventeenth century.

We have the basic outlines in place, sufficient for our purpose, which is to seek to understand the transformation that will take place once the "man who outshone the Sun King" is forced to endure years of harsh imprisonment. We are able, as noted above, to reconstruct Fouquet's state of mind through writings unavailable to public view at that time, composed during his imprisonment.

Collaterally, we have full access to a document that was available to the public during this same period and that was indeed consulted widely. The breadth of its subsequent translation into all major languages testifies to its staying power in the public's eyes. And, as we shall see, what this volume had to say was significant in its own right concerning "such Maxims of Solomon as are Necessary for the prudent Conduct of Life," but significant most particularly because to the public eye the author was none other than this same Fouquet.

That this is so means we are in a position to see how the masses viewed the fate of Fouquet. What did the years that followed closely on the death of Fouquet have to say about him and his imprisonment?

As we have noted, the preface to the 1677 French original, appearing three years before what would be the death of Fouquet, seeks to give us the setting of the work's composition and the frame of mind of the author. Whatever the intent of the actual author—if that is the best way to put it for now—in giving the "Counsels of Wisdom from Solomon" to be reflected upon by this unnamed individual, the effect was immediate and unequivocal. Here we are presented with none other than the reflections from the erstwhile Superintendent of Finances, Monsieur Fouquet, writing from prison in Pignerol, and as of 1677 now in prison for fifteen years.

Here is just a bit of the flavor of the preface:

> Il y a longtemps, Theotime, que vous me faites la grâce de me plaindre, et de sentir pour moi les peines de ma solitude. J'ai pris souvent la liberté de vous répondre, que ce n'est pas un malheur d'être inconnu: permettez que je vous témoigne aujourd'hui que j'aurais tort de m'ennuyer, et que je suis avec un homme qui vaut bien toutes les compagnies que je pourrais voir.
>
> J'ose au moins vous dire, que depuis j'ai le bonheur de le posséder, les tristes spectacles et le silence affreux du désert ou la fortune me retient encore, n'empêchent pas que les heures n'y passent bien vite et que le temps ne soit une des choses qui y manquent.

Rather than translate myself, as I want to turn to an early English edition in this chapter, I will let that volume do the job.

> It is long since, Theotimus, that you were so kind as to compassionate my State of Life, and even to feel the Inconveniences of Solitude upon my account, that I have often taken the Freedom to tell you, that I never esteemed it a Misfortune to live retired from the World: give me leave, once again, to assure you, that I should be to blame, if I shewed any Concern at my present Circumstances, since I am so happy, as to enjoy a Person, the most engaging of any I ever could be blessed with.
>
> This at least I will be bold to say, that since I have been so fortunate, as to contract this Acquaintance, neither the Solitariness of the Place I am stilled detained in by Providence, nor the melancholy Objects that surround me on all sides, hinder my hours from flowing agreeably; and that Time itself is one of the Things I grow most covetous of.[1]

[1] Michel Boutauld, *The Counsels of Wisdom, or, A Collection of such Maxims of Solomon as are Most Necessary for the prudent Conduct of Life: With Proper Reflections upon them. Written Originally in French by Monseigneur Fouquet, Sometime Lord High Treasurer of France, in the Reign of Lewis XIV,* done into English by a Gent, with some Account of the Illustrious Author (Oxford, 1736).

To review, we have several leads to follow as we evaluate Fouquet in relation to Koheleth and Ecclesiastes, which is our larger purpose. (1) What we are now able to see of his own writings in Pignerol. (2) What *Conseils* purports to show us. (3) What editions appearing soon after his death offer as commendations in his name, and the historical angle of vision they choose to highlight in setting this forth.

Items 1 and 3 are uncontroversial. They are what they are. If one judges the attribution to Fouquet as in error, it remains of interest to see what these editions want us to know about him all the same. They operate on a plane of history in which Fouquet lives on as a major figure, dramatically cast into prison for a great portion of his life, where he would die. After this his memory, as they say, lives on. In England, the flirtation with absolute monarchy during the reign of Charles I, and then after the Restoration in the person of Charles II, means that any take on Fouquet and Louis XIV will have that coloration and that historical particularity. But that does not prevent us from seeing what someone sympathetic to his dire fate, and what are taken to be his reflections written during this time, might choose to highlight.

As for item 2, *Conseils* has chosen to make its author the famous man in exile, whose memory in 1677 is also "living on" during his imprisonment. Historians make it clear that, in addition to the direct correspondence between Paris and the Royal Jailor (the same figure made famous in the "Man in the Iron Mask" stories, one Benigné Dauvergne de Saint-Mars), concerning Fouquet and other prisoners, the general public had not forgotten about this man. In the latter years of his imprisonment, the king allowed his wife and his children to visit him. And Fouquet also shared the royal prison with a man still very much significant in the affairs of the court, Antonin Nompar de Caumont, 1st Duke of Lauzun, due to the ongoing love and inheritance issues he evoked. So when *Conseils* appears in published form in 1677, the preface's apparent purpose is achieved. Fouquet is given voice through the vehicle of the sentence-based wisdom of King Solomon.

I want to reproduce here the long opening commendation of Monsieur Fouquet as given by the translator of *Conseils*, one J. Leake (he is addressing Charles Butler, Earl of Arran and chancellor of the University of Oxford). This is the picture the public has of him fifty-six years after his death at Pignerol. We get to see how his imprisonment is being viewed as well as the reasons given for it.

The Counsels of Wisdom, or, A Collection of such Maxims of Solomon as are Most Necessary for the prudent Conduct of Life: With Proper Reflections upon them. Written Originally in French by Monseigneur Fouquet, Sometime Lord High Treasurer of France, in the Reign of Lewis XIV. Done into English by a Gent. With some Account of the Illustrious Author (Oxford, 1736).[2]

> Prefatory Discourse Giving some Account of the Illustrious Author.
>
> My Lord, The Illustrious Superintendent Fouquet, so famous for his Disgrace, Exile, and long Imprisonment . . . was the author of *The Counsels of Wisdom.* A Book, if the Opinion of F. Bouhours may have any Weight with your Lordship, and the Reader, that is so well, and so elegantly written, that none of the like Kind can claim a Preference to it: it may serve, He says, to improve our Morals, and our Stile at the same Time, and no One but this celebrated Writer, who was so considerable by his Birth, as well as Perfect Merit, could have been so proper an Interpreter of the Sentiments of Solomon, as He. As for the Language, it was necessary to understand it, as well as this illustrious Recluse did, to make it so universally esteem'd as a Pattern of Eloquence, by the Generality of the French Nations. *Entretien sur la Langue Française*, p. 166.

[2] The full text of this edition is available on Google Books.

Here there is a brief discourse on whether solitude or action are better contexts for contemplation and the kind of reflections we can read in this volume:

> But to return to the Author: The Occasion, my Lord, of the Treasurer's misfortunes, was the Jealousy, of his ambitious Rival Monsieur Colbert. He happen'd to despise too much a Man of low Birth, whom he knew not to be so great a Person by his singular Talents and Qualifications. Monsieur Fouquet's Reflections upon the XIII's Maxim of the third Part of this Book, are a clear proof of this Assertion: There we find him expressing himself after the following Manner.

He begins immediately with the theme of jealousy, attributed to Colbert, who was undoubtedly plotting to bring Fouquet down and who would become his replacement:

> Whenever you see Persons of mean Parentage, without Understanding or Merit, exalted to Posts, that you imagine you have a Right to; don't quarrel with Heaven or Providence about it: Remember, 'tis the noblest Instance of your Courage, to be able and willing to suppress the Motions of Anger and Jealousy, that are apt to arise in the human Breast on such Occasions.

This section continues for several paragraphs; the point is that the translator sees one section of *Counsels* as directly arising from the transfer of authority from Fouquet to Colbert, and the former's decline and imprisonment occasioned by the latter—what Fouquet perceived as a grave injustice.

> My Lord, Since Monsieur Fouquet's Disgrace the Office of High Treasurer of France, which was Hereditary, has been abolish'd; as had been before that of High Constable, in the family of Montmorency. It seems, these great Officers were neither of them accountable for their Administrations, and consequently, formidable to a

> young ambitious Prince, who was resolved to be Master, as well as Father of his People: if he sometimes forgot the latter, 'twas owing to Inadvertence, rather than to any settled Cruelty of Temper. Lewis XIV tho' then a young Monarch, understood the great Secret of Government, *never to let his Ministers be too powerful.* And it was owing to this Sentiment, as well as to what has been hinted at before, that the Superintendent fell a Sacrifice to this Prince's Jealousy; and the absoluteness of his Office found its final Period at the same Time.

Leake is speaking here about Louis XIV's reasons for going after Fouquet, including his own personal jealousy, which in turn led to his absolutism as monarch.

> His Lordship never discusses any mean Thing; but he spent his Money, perhaps in a too popular, and sometimes too splendid a Manner. However, Adversity made him think soberly, and embrace such Precepts which Prosperity, and an affluent Fortune, had him forget too much.

Here then is Leake's own sympathetic judgment of Fouquet's error. And this launches a long discourse about adversity and its potential for transforming men in general and Fouquet in particular. He does not quote any of the reflections in a specific way, and so we might judge this rumination as the drift of both them and what he regards as the transformed attitude of Fouquet he wishes to commend.

> And this need not be any Manner of Wonder or Astonishment to us: for if we would deal faithfully with Ourselves and the World, and acknowledge what Benefits we reap in the School of Adversity, we should easily assent to this Truth. 'Tis there we learnt to correct the Follies and Infirmities of our Nature; and how to improve the Faculties of our Mind and Understanding; by which we always become more acceptable to God and Man. King David's Assertion, that it was good that he had been afflicted;

would not then seem so great a Paradox to the Generality, if we did but humbly submit to, and make a proper Use of the like wholesome Discipline: our Illustrious Author is an amiable Instance of the wonderful Efficacy of such a Practice. Adversity presented to him all his Infirmities in a true Mirrour; he discover'd his Pride and his Passion in their proper Colours, which appear'd before to him as the Dress of Power and Grandeur. The greater and higher Persons are in Place and Dignity, the more they stand in need of the Sovereign Remembrancer. Mean and inferior People have their Faults as often told them as they commit them, and sometimes oftener. The Counsels of Friends, the Emulation, Envy, and Opposition of Equals, the malice of their Enemies, and the Authority and Prejudice of their Superiors will often present their Defects to them, and interrupt any Career of their Vanity or Passion: but Princes and great Men, who generally can have but few Friends, (because Friendship presupposes some Kind of Equality) their Counsellors, I say, are too commonly Compliers with their Humours, and Flatterers of their Infirmities. Observation and Experience are never so pregnant and convincing as under Adversity; that refreshes the Memory, makes it revolve what was purposely laid aside, that it might never be remember'd more: It reforms and sharpens the Understanding, and faithfully collects all that had been left undone, or done amiss, and presents it to the Judgment; which now the Clouds and Mists of Pride and Flattery are dispers'd, discerns what Misfortunes attend those Faults; the Gradation and Progress each Error hath made, and how close the Punishment hath attended the Transgression. Besides, were there no other good to be expected from Adversity than what keeps it Company; if we were not allur'd by well bearing it, to be freed from, and rewarded for it; the present Benefit and Advantage it gives us, and entitles us to, renders it a State often much to be desired; It gives us a Claim to the Compassion of all good Men: To him that is afflicted Pity should be shew'd from his Friend, says Job 6.4. Nay, it gives us a Title to Salvation itself; for Thou wilt save the afflicted People, says the Psalmist: nay, a greater Person than these, says, happy are ye, if ye suffer for Righteousness Sake. Yet notwithstanding all these Invitations and Promises, all the Examples of good men, and Blessings which have crown'd those Examples; all our own Experience of Ourselves, that we have really gain'd more Piety in one Year's affliction, than the whole Course of our prosperous Fortunes, we are so far from a Habit of Patience, and so weary of Sufferings, that we are even ready to barter away our Innocence, to better our Condition.

Our great Author indeed seems to have been so far influenc'd by the former Part of the reasoning upon this Head, that he stood entirely clear from the Malignancy of the Conclusion. I shall venture, My Lord, to give your Lordship and the Reader a few of his religious Sentiments upon the Argument; and, I hope, neither will take the Anticipation amiss.

Accustom yourself, says he, to look upon every Thing that happens with a thorough Resignation. When Affliction or Adversity is your Lot, grow not angry with God Almighty, neither quit your Resolution of remaining always faithful to Him. Bear His Chastisements with Lowliness and Humility, and never let your Courage or Virtue sink under the Trial. Remember that God chastens every one whom He loves. And as a Father is never better pleas'd with his Child, that when he receives Correction submissively at his Hands, so Man is never so acceptable to his Creator, as when he appears humble, obedient, and faithful under His afflicting Rod. There is no man exempt from Suffering; the true Christian suffers with Patience, and the Saint with Pleasure.

This, without doubt is the highest Stage of the spiritual Life; and I may say, after the holy Fathers, that to see a Person enjoy a heavenly Calm of Soul amidst the Ruins

> and Distress of his Fortune, is to behold what is most wonderful, under the new and powerful Dispensation of the Incarnate Word: to hear, I say, that this very Person has no other Complaints to make to those who visit upon him, nor to the Holy Angels who look down upon him, than what St. Paul had, when he suffer'd in the Flesh, and declar'd that he rejoyc'd with exceeding great Joy! Nay, that he was over-whelm'd with it; and the Satisfaction he felt, greatly surpass'd his Pains and Penalties. Now these were the Sentiments of all the Primitive Saints: they always spoke of the Time of Adversity, as the most happy and improveable Period of their whole Lives.
>
> In short; by our Sufferings we resemble our Crucified Saviour whilst on Earth; we enrole Ourselves in the glorious Army of Martyrs in Heaven; and in our Death, transcend the very Angelic Host: to die, and to suffer, is the highest Pitch of Glory, that God-Man attain'd, when He fulfill'd all Love, and amidst the Terrors of Death upon the Cross, pronounc'd aloud, It is finished!

The discourse on Adversity as Teacher, given with rhetorical skill and force, concludes here. We return to Leake's presuppositions about the conditions of Fouquet's imprisonment:

> My Lord, Our Author wrote these Reflections during his Confinement: and he tells a Friend, the Reason which prompted him to this Undertaking, was the Solitariness of the Place in which he then was; however melancholy as it is, or as it seems to be in your Apprehension, he declares, he cannot but think it the most convenient Place in the World, to meditate and ruminate upon the Writings of King Solomon. This I affirm, says he, even upon the Supposition I entertain'd upon my last reading this Sacred Writer; that the Author of Wisdom, who dictated these Proverbs to him in his Retirement, will not please to open or explain them to any Persons, who do not first ask it of him, and even put themselves, into such similar solitary Circumstances he did, by retiring

from the Hurry and Bustle of the World; those great Enemies to the Attention, as well as the Pleasure of those, who are willing and ready to embrace Instruction.

If I have but done Justice to my great Author in the Translation, I shall think myself happy in having given to the English Reader, a most judicious and instructive System of Christian Morality. If this degenerate Age were capable of any Reformation in that Respect, this Treatise one would think, might contribute largely to it: but, with Sorrow I write it, I fear Nothing can effect such a Change, but that Power which created the World, and will raise the Dead!

This brings to a close the opening commendation. As stated, he isn't using the occasion to call to mind the specific maxims of the volume to follow, but rather is giving us a portrait of Fouquet based upon what one might reasonably conclude was at the center of this thinking: How a man of high estate fell, why, and what was he able to learn through adversity about deeper spiritual realities. He omits to say anything about death itself, but we can infer that this fact is simply too well known and obvious to call specific attention to it.

What is striking is the degree to which what the translator writes in this discourse is in fact fully consistent with what we can consult about Fouquet's thinking in his last years in Pignerol, during which time he was given paper and allowed to write at his leisure. So if the translator, and the general public at large, are in error to think *Conseils* was his own work, all the more remarkable then is the complete agreement of the portrait we have just been given with the (undisputed) writings that have come down to us from his own pen.

We will turn to the specifics of that below.

For now let it be simply noted that the final chapter of Ecclesiastes, treated above, gives evidence of being something like the final words of Koheleth, its protagonist and the "single brooding consciousness" that permeates the eleven chapters preceding. Ecclesiastes, at its front end, provides us a glimpse at the "author" not unlike in purpose to the preface of *Conseils*. It says just enough to establish an association with Solomon without belaboring the point through exact correspondence with the long account of him given in chapters 1–11 of the first book of Kings. Indeed, the brevity of the referentiality and what it chooses to highlight will very quickly give way to the main contents of the book itself. However clipped, evocative, and oblique this autobiographical glimpse is, it will have served its purpose merely by giving us a point of view in something of the same way the brief preface of *Conseils* does.

For very different reasons, it has become impossible to consider the twelve-chapter book of Ecclesiastes as written by Solomon—a debate that ended (if that is the right word) in critical scholarship in the nineteenth century. Indeed, one might wonder what kind of concrete account of authorship such a view was being asked to rely on. So, too, one might say, the large-scale production of *Conseils* has a certain genre independence and life of its own that belongs to how it moves along, with selections of maxims, paraphrases, and thoughtful reflections. We may on the basis of information known to us (but unknown to the first readers in France in the years before Fouquet's death) question how Fouquet might reasonably be the author of such a grand composition—not least from records that monitor closely how and under what conditions he may write at all. Only in the final years of his imprisonment is he able to put pen to paper. This comes in the form of personal correspondence with his wife and his mother, official responses to queries being made of him by the Secretary of War and Louis XIV, and some scattered spiritual writings. That is all.

But there is sufficient enough of the latter to bring alongside what we have been chronicling thus far, as seen in the rich testimony from the 1736 English translation of *Conseils*.

4
Koheleth's Solomonic Meditation

I have chosen the chapter title with forethought. Much of my discussion to follow will be an explanation of that. Ecclesiastes, more than many other books, requires the proper starting point. The proper angle of vision. It needs a reader coming to it with the right kind of expectations. In that way the reader will read the book properly and find the book reading him or her. The idea of reading any biblical text—or any text—neutrally is just naive. We have to know where we are going when we start to go.

The book of Ecclesiastes has a protagonist. Not an intermittent one. Not one sharing the stage with others (though this has sometimes been argued to account for the changing views we encounter—that is, the protagonist is shadowboxing with real or imagined opponents, a view that has now largely disappeared). No, the book does not make this an obvious feature at all. The one protagonist introduced as simply "Koheleth" never for a moment leaves the stage. One insightful critic calls this feature of the book what sets it apart from other OT books. Ecclesiastes places before us "a single brooding consciousness," as he characterizes it.[1] He is introduced at the start, and all that

[1] Michael V. Fox, "Aging and Death in Qoheleth 12," *JSOT* 42 (1988): 55–77; idem, *Ecclesiastes: The Traditional Hebrew Text with the New JPS Translation*, JPS Bible Commentary (Jewish Publication Society, 2004); idem, *A Time to Tear Down and a Time to Build Up: A Rereading of Ecclesiastes* (Eerdmans, 1999).

follows is his brooding self, inhabiting every single verse, until we exit the book at what sounds like his dying last words.

So who is this Koheleth? His name is enigmatic. It seems to point to a function as much as a personal name, so much so that he can even be called "*the* Koheleth" at one juncture. Who he is then is tied up with what he does. Is defined by that. So now to what it means to "koheleth." The verb in Hebrew has to do with collecting or assembling.[2] We might think of this as assembling maxims, wise if difficult sayings. That makes a lot of sense. Yet when this vocation of Koheleth is described at the close of the book by a narrator, the activity of collecting wisdom does not use that verb form. And the verb is never used in that sense in the book.

The alternative is to think of Koheleth as gathering people or, relatedly, gathering not things like wisdom only, but riches, wives, property. Negative, garish, pointless accumulation. As when people cry out for manna and quails and get so much it comes out of their nostrils, or, when stored, goes foul. The tradition had in mind the gathering of people when it spoke of the Ecclesiast, or, following Luther, the Preacher, as in one who gathers a solemn assembly, an ecclesia. Yet it may be that this more positive role is intended to sit uneasily alongside the notion of vain accumulation. The Accumulator who more properly ought to be the Ecclesiast. A proper role gone vainly wrong, as the book will show it.[3]

I want to park the discussion on this point for now, so as to underscore the second item in the title. Koheleth's *Solomonic*

2 It also is related to a nominal-form *qahal*, typically meaning "assembly" or "congregation," and hence Luther's preference for *Das Prediger*, "The Preacher."

3 I deal with these matters in further detail in "A Canonical Reading of Ecclesiastes," in *Acts of Interpretation: Scripture, Theology, and Culture*, ed. S. A. Cummins and Jens Zimmerman (Eerdmans, 2018). I believe the name Koheleth was chosen due to the frequent occurrence of forms of the verb found in 1 Kings 8, where Solomon "gathers" the people. The author relied on this chapter in the narratives about Solomon to construct a name for the protagonist of his work. He is the Koheleth, the one who collects, gathers, assembles, accumulates, as part and parcel of his identity.

Meditation. I will refer to something like a Solomonic trio as preferable to classifications of recent scholarship like "wisdom literature," and will say more about that in a later chapter. Ecclesiastes is in some way related to Solomon by virtue of its close association with Proverbs and Song of Songs. But the key here is "in some way." Those books make the link crystal clear. The titles set it out unmistakably. Our book only flirts with it, or is content to register it by means of the trio idea, in terms of its placement alongside other books in the canon. The book itself never uses the name Solomon. "Koheleth" is how it wishes to speak of the single brooding consciousness. Koheleth has been a king in Jerusalem. With that come all the proper associations we might have of a temptation to overaccumulate, and Solomon could fit the bill. But it cannot be an accident that the book chooses not to name him. It belongs to its intention to evoke Solomon while letting Koheleth be himself. Hence, Koheleth's *Solomonic*—adjective, not noun—Meditation. The book is adjectivally a Solomonic work, not nominally a work of Solomon.

The ancients also recognized this fact (Origen, Gregory of Nyssa, Didymus). They saw the association, but more significantly saw the omission of the name as critical to proper interpretation. Didymus puts it this way.

> Actually the Spirit is the author of the divinely inspired Scriptures . . . Either the real author is Solomon, or [some] other wise man may have written it. Maybe we should opt for the latter so that nobody may say the speaker talks about himself.[4]

The idea of "authorship," debated with high seriousness in recent centuries, failed properly to understand the character of, the nature of, the book's studied association with Solomon. To introduce registers like "authentic" or "fictional" fails to take

[4] Didymus the Blind, *Commentary on Ecclesiastes* 7.9, in *Proverbs, Ecclesiastes, Song of Solomon*, ed. J. Robert Wright, ACCS 9 (IVP Academic, 2005), 192.

seriously what is *not* being said by the book. This is Koheleth's book, and we grasp how it is Solomonic only by attending to what it has to say and the manner in which it says it. An evocation is what we are dealing with, and this has nothing to do with authorship in the manner debated in modernity. The arguments for the late date of the book, due to the history of the Hebrew language, are correct in their own way, but may equally mislead us as to their ultimate utility. If they fail to let the book be Solomonic by evocation, they are as untrue to the canonical presentation as those who insist it was the king penning a story about himself in some modern sense, like unto autobiography. Relevant here, incidentally, and to be developed further, is the similar attribution of *Conseils* to the well-known Nicolas Fouquet.

And that brings us nicely to the third term of the title. Meditation. I would be open to alternatives, but the word "meditation" on my ear suggests a combination of (1) instruction—that is, something didactic in intention; (2) rumination—that is, something that goes over the same territory again and again because one is trying to find their way, because the terrain is rough, because the subject matter resists objective formulation and resolution (more to the point, this "single brooding consciousness" at work); and (3) confession. Confession in the sense of recognizing that God must be addressed as the proprietor of true wisdom, that one cannot accumulate this but beg for it as a gift, and this only after failure and a grim face-to-face encounter with one's pride and vanity.

If all this is on the right track, we need now to come to terms with how we should approach the translation of the main thematic word of the book, its brooding distillate. *Hebel, hebelim.* Now there are roughly three options one will note in commentaries.[5] "Absurd." This suggests that something outside of Koheleth is fundamentally awry, and cantankerously,

[5] See my discussion in Seitz, "Canonical Reading of Ecclesiastes."

infuriatingly so. Creation (to use religious language) is awry, and that creates the riposte: *Absurd!* This fits nicely inside the wisdom-literature model of increasing pessimism in the movement from Proverbs, to Job, to Ecclesiastes, and often works in tandem with it.

Another possibility is "transient" or "fleeting." This is better, closer to the ground root of the word, having to do with breath or vapor. Exhale. CO_2. Lacking generative potential. But like "absurd," it keeps the characterization at some distance from Koheleth himself. Yes, the world itself is fleeting, *Hebel.*

Like the word "Abel" (a proper name similar to the adjectival form *hebel*): here today and gone tomorrow.

But I prefer "ungraspable," in the sense that what Koheleth wants to assemble and organize defeats his efforts, and purposely so. Hence his Solomonic meditation, rumination, and confession. It is for this reason that those who now argue for a genuine structure and design to the book—one admittedly not easy to see—are right. A single brooding consciousness that broods toward something, probably not obvious even to himself, and which finally reaches a goal. A goal ironically established by surrender and confession: a letting go. The accumulator in a position to be an ecclesiast after all, gathering people before the admonition: "Fear God, keep his commandments." That is what it means to have had life. As wisdom has a beginning in the fear of the Lord (in Proverbs), so too it has an end. "The end of the matter, all has been heard. Fear God and keep his commandments." Koheleth has shared his Solomonic meditation and shown himself in the end to be wise through trial and surrender. The one who had it all has nothing; the one who has nothing finds everything.

At this point I want to do a walk-through of the book, choosing select passages to illustrate key features of the book's design and overall intention.

First: The angle of vision the book asks us to follow is of a Solomon in old age and a Solomon whose gaze is retrospective and, in light of that, pedagogically driven.

The end of the book makes that crystal clear, and I will turn to the text in a moment. But it can be seen elsewhere as well, and the book assumes the single brooding consciousness is looking back on things. *Has* learned his lesson. This is what tinges the meditation with a confessional tone. The opening chapters have Koheleth describe his grand building and amassing and conclude about it, as something behind him now, that it was *hebel*. The tone of the book is of having tried things out and finding out the real story in the end.

The distinct sense of old age and approaching death is conveyed at the close. A world is coming to end—Koheleth's own world. He reaches out to admonish. Final words are always pregnant and heavy laden, and especially these of Koheleth.

Many like to speak of an epilogue beginning at 12:9. It is obvious enough that Koheleth has stopped speaking and is being spoken about. But the language of "epilogue" is often invoked to declare the last verses a correction of something too extreme, even an effort to secure a hearing by means of redirecting what he has said. But when one understands the final section as the very place the book has been heading and the place of aged retrospection with which the book starts, then the idea of discordance is shown to be false. Precisely in his sober approach to death and in his newly (if finally) acquired upper-level wisdom, he is commendable. He has come to teach us. Wisdom has a beginning in the fear of the LORD, and so too it has an end. This is life as such. Life, to quote Koheleth, "under the sun."

I have referred to the beginning of the book, and so I will go there now. As indicated, often the epilogue is called a framing device, negotiating an uncooperative or unorthodox Koheleth by speaking over his head to the reader. We do not agree with the evaluation even as we accept the notion of a frame supplied by editors, which means to link the book to Proverbs.[6]

Rarely does one use the same terminology to speak of a frame on the front end of the book, since the technique is more subtle. It is notable that Koheleth's clear stepping onto the stage does not happen until twelve verses into the first chapter. "I Koheleth was king over Israel." Therewith begins a thirty-three-verse soliloquy running to the end of chapter 2, which orients the "single brooding consciousness" to follow.

"Frame" could mean to point to the obvious symmetry of verse 2 and the final refrain at 12:9. But this leaves out the so-called epilogue. Support for this idea depends on just how we understand the opening verses of chapter 1, prior to the obvious introduction of Koheleth as king over Israel at 1:12. Along with select others, this section deserves to be called a framing section in that it sets up the conditions against which the book tends to push. This is what allows us properly to see the confessional tone of Koheleth's retrospection. He has broken the rules.

There is not time to unpack the meaning of these opening verses in a line-by-line commentary. I will take this up in a chapter to follow.

This much must be grasped. This is not a poem about the futility of the created order. The opposite is the case.[7] The movement of creation bears witness to the order and majesty of God's providential design. Its closest analogy is found, unsurprisingly, in the divine verdict after the flood. The rainbow is its heavenly seal and bond. God has planted a bulwark against the flood. The sun runs like a champion and to its place it returns again. Here the Psalms' extolling of creative protection and power rhymes

[6] Michael V. Fox, "Frame Narrative and Composition in the Book of Qoheleth," *HUCA* 48 (1977): 83–106; Gerald H. Wilson, "'The Words of the Wise': The Intent and Significance of Qoheleth 12:9–14," *JBL* 103, no. 2 (1984): 175–92.

[7] I discuss this in greater detail in "Canonical Reading of Ecclesiastes." Compare the discussion in Mette Bundvad, *Time in the Book of Ecclesiastes* (Oxford University Press, 2015).

with Genesis and Ecclesiastes. The proper translation of verse 8 is not "all *things* are *hebel*," but "all *words* are *hebel*." The earth remains forever. Sun, seas, rivers, winds move on their divinely given courses. Human comprehension, not so much. We forget. We use words to explain, but cannot fathom the divine mind and will. That is life "under the sun," east of Eden.

The trouble comes, we learn very quickly, in trying to live outside these bounds. Recently it has been very helpfully observed that Koheleth's grand experiment, upon which he looks ruefully backward, has again taken its cues directly from Genesis. "'Let there be light'; and there was light. And God saw that the light was good," is here under usurpation by a godlike Koheleth. Let there be gardens, and riches, and grand, frenzied building; and Koheleth "looked and I saw that it was *hebel*." This is not a bitter account of why bad things happen to good people. It is a conscious self-parodying by someone who had sought to break the rules set down by God in the wake of Eden, and now ruefully takes note of that folly.[8]

To state it again: Koheleth's self-description in the clothing of super Solomon is self-parodying; it is not meant as photographic recounting of his acquisitional self but rather intentionally focuses on and aggrandizes events for pedagogical purpose: in order to display a sober, penitential grasp of things, now looking back. "I did all these things and at the time they seemed grand and they were grand. But now I see them as so much *hebel* because I am looking at them through different, wiser eyes."

In that sense, and to summarize, one can speak of an omniscient frame in place, at the beginning (1:1–11) and at the end. We are told what the state of affairs is concerning the world in which Koheleth does his reflecting at the start, and are meant to see this transgressed by what Koheleth describes immediately following (1:12–2:26). This is how Koheleth means to teach us: I tried this way. Do not do the same.

[8] Arian Verheij, "Paradise Retried: On Qoheleth 2:4–6," *JSOT* 50 (1991): 113–15.

The final framing, in what is called the epilogue (12:9–14), confirms that Koheleth was reliable, he taught in a tough way, and his words are a mature bookend on the enterprise called wisdom. Solomon the young composed proverbs. Rules of the road. Koheleth's Solomonic meditation shows us exceptions to the rules. Proverbs introduces the paradigms, which like all grammars have to simplify to get started. Strong verbs appear first. But strong verbs are often verbs we really do not use frequently in life. Weak verbs, in all languages, are really the verbs we use day to day. They are the thick words that live in life deep down.

The sayings of the wise are like goads, sharp-edged in order to get our attention and to steer us, often against our wills. Koheleth tried this way. He learned a lesson, and he imparts his wisdom as he approaches death. Here is what Martin Luther called the "theological use of the Law," that which breaks us on its wheel that our eyes might be redirected and lifted to our Creator. Wisdom had a beginning in Proverbs, and it has an end here: "The end of the matter, all has been heard, beware of any beyond these."

I have argued in another place that the Fourth Gospel reiterates this idea when, like Koheleth, it draws to a close. It is always hard to identify borrowing. We can at least say, however, great minds think alike. "Of making many books there is no end" (Eccl 12:12). "There are also many other things which Jesus did; were every one of them to be written, I suppose that the world itself could not contain the books that would be written" (John 21:25). That is not intended as a positive image, in the romantic sense of "what a great man and what an impossible task to write it all down." No, this take tracks better with Koheleth's ending and is truer to John's intent:[9] "These things have been written. They are sufficient. More information is not needed to convey what God wants

[9] Christopher R. Seitz, "Booked Up: Ending John and Ending Jesus," in *Figured Out: Typology and Providence in Christian Scripture* (Westminster John Knox, 2001), 91–102.

to convey in the record provided about his Son. All has been heard. Fear God and keep the commandments of his Son." There is a Johannine rhyming with Ecclesiastes.

So much for beginning and ending. But what about middle? What about larger design?[10] One can ask a similar question about the structure of Job. Why are there three rounds of comforters? Are they just repeating themselves, or is there movement we can detect?

Oddly enough, in all of the efforts to describe the contents of Ecclesiastes as it moves across its twelve chapters, one finding has endured. Most agree there is a marked middle, located at chapter 6. The refrains having to do with *hebel* and chasing after wind only appear in the first half of the book, and then cease. Koheleth gets tired of chasing, sees the pointlessness of it, as it were. The book's structure says this by implication. So what replaces this in part 2? A sobered search for a different species of wisdom. These two thematic features only loosely organize, or reside within, the halves of the books.[11]

Bundvad and Christianson have concluded from this fact that the effect is intentionally built into the book: Ecclesiastes presents loosely organized ruminations.[12] Koheleth has run up against an epistemological block he once tried to escape, and he is trying to get used to his new place of standing. It is uncomfortable, like trying to get sea legs after a life on land. Striving after wind is what it means to be searching for something you cannot and are not meant to grasp. Eventually that wind blows itself out.

[10] See Christopher R. Seitz, "Job: Full Structure, Movement, and Interpretation," *Int* 43 (1989): 5–17.

[11] Addison G. Wright, "The Riddle of the Sphinx: The Structure of the Book of Qoheleth," *CBQ* 30 (1968): 313–34; "The Riddle of the Sphinx Revisited: Numerical Patterns in Qoheleth," *CBQ* 45 (1983): 32–43.

[12] Bundvad, *Time in the Book of Qoheleth*; Eric Christianson, *A Time to Tell: Narrative Strategies in Ecclesiastes* (Sheffield Academic, 1998).

The tone of part 2 is more questioning in character. "Who knows?" is the theme or motto. Koheleth is less sure-footed in his frustration and indignation. This has been taken to align with part 1 in the sense that it is just another form of despair. A kind of hopelessness or enigmatic resignation. But this is to ignore an obvious structural distinction marked by a clear change of direction and terminology in part 2.

One feature that has also been insufficiently appreciated is the presence of the proverb form. Koheleth is citing wisdom in an authoritative way, even as it is a wisdom more probing and complicated. Certain things cannot be fathomed. That too is wisdom. Epistemic blockage is okay. The world cannot be figured out. "What is crooked cannot be made straight" is not an indictment of the Good God. It is simply paying tribute to a created reality that cannot be figured out. One can observe in nature certain curiosities beyond human comprehension.

As an aside, when I taught at St Andrews we shared a courtyard with the psychology school. Its most prominent professor had spent his entire life studying bird songs. Why do birds sing? Theory after theory has been proposed. He was the expert. His conclusion? We do not know. That did not depress him or make him any less the expert. It did make him wise.

I am not sure it has been sufficiently noted how this tone—*advanced wisdom*, shall we call it—lines up with the book of Job. Job begins to shoot back against the friends' wisdom with his own in round three. They fizzle out. Job is treated to a divine display of created mystery—animals out beyond human organization and domestication—that signals to him he is truly in the presence of the God who created animals before he breathed life into mankind.[13]

There is a further structural feature to which a good deal of attention has been paid. The so-called joy refrains. These significantly span both parts of the book. They are its drumbeat.

[13] See my treatment in *The Heights of the Hills Are His Also* (Baylor University Press, 2024).

This is not to say they drown out the darker music, the minor notes. They definitely do not. But neither can they be called *carpe diem* in the manner of some.[14] *Carpe diem* is at root a very dark account of things, just to the degree it assumes one has no enduring hope in God's created goodness or plan. Koheleth is not turning to the bottle to numb out life or indulging in cheap despair. A middle finger to the sky. The reason the drumbeat continues is not to offset this and that dark utterance but consists in the total effect achieved.

Here an important point needs to be made about Ecclesiastes's peculiar form of discourse. I have mentioned its ruminating character already. At times it seems to be like waves lapping on a shore. It is far closer in form to Lamentations or Song of Songs in lacking distinct narrative purpose. It is a single brooding consciousness, and brooding does not lend itself to weights and measurement.

A quantitative approach to reading the book—measuring the thickness of its despair or its contradictory mode, as against commendations to enjoy—will not do proper justice to the intention of the canonical form, even as they are tempting integers as one reads along. Something is going on that requires patience fully to understand. As at the bed of a dying soul, the incoherence and back-and-forth resist tidy evaluation. What one does not want to do is dismiss the commendations to joy and life when suddenly they burst on the scene, as though they were simply outweighed by the sum of the struggle itself and therefore incongruous grasping at straws. In such a context they weigh more, not less, simply by virtue of their persistence and their surprising irruption when they speak forth.

Perhaps too much has been made of their getting bigger as we read along. Koheleth, "Preacher of Joy," may be an attempt

[14] Among others, see Tremper Longman, *The Book of Ecclesiastes*, NICOT (Eerdmans, 1998).

to say too much.[15] "Confessions of a Workaholic" was another label given to this, as a process of detoxing begins to gain ground.[16] Whatever their limitations, these takes are surely more honest about a distinct theme and reality built into the book than those who dismiss the sayings as mere "seize the day" numbing agents.

In this vein I think it is critical to observe the location and size of the final one. It does not come at just any point in part 2 of the book, but is positioned just before the final, funereal adieu. And preceded by the proverbial appeal to loosen one's grip in life. Mr. Control and Acquisition is here a very different man.

As we are coming to the end, and the word *hebel* appears here and just before the epilogue, it is important to be sure any translation does not overdetermine the meaning. *Hebel* is the thematic word of the book as a whole. Nyssa said it was a word without referentiality, that is, its utterance was itself, without direct semantic meaning.[17] Vapor incarnated by moving the air in uttering the phoneme *hebel*. If one wants a semantic equivalent—the alternative being to transliterate *hebel* into English—it must be against this conceptual backdrop. *Hebel* is Abel; here for a moment and then gone. *Hebel* is chasing after wind, something that can't be held. *Hebel* is "You can't take it with you"—"You can't comprehend it"—"You are up against a world in which God is forever, and creation is his own sovereign domain." *Hebel* means "finally ungraspable by God's creatures."

15 Norman R. Whybray, "Qoheleth, Preacher of Joy," *JSOT* 23 (1982): 87–98. See also Eunny P. Lee, *The Vitality of Enjoyment in Qoheleth's Theological Rhetoric*, BZAW 353 (de Gruyter, 2005).

16 Robert K. Johnston, "Confessions of a Workaholic: A Reappraisal of Qoheleth," *CBQ* 38 (1976): 14–28.

17 Gregory of Nyssa, *Scholia on Ecclesiastes* 2.1.2.

The final appeal to joy is indeed longer, its position critical to the total intention of the book as a whole. It is a speech-act, as is now said.

Listen to these key verses. They introduce the final refrain. On previous occasions the fact that the refrains sit uneasily in their immediate context has been grounds for regarding them as disjunctive, mitigations, seize-the-day qualifications of an otherwise somber discourse.

The final refrain is not disjunctive but continuous with the tone of the verses that precede. Koheleth is about to say goodbye to us. These words are weighty given their position in the book.

11 [1] Cast your bread upon the waters,
for you will find it after many days.
[2] Give a portion to seven, or even to eight,
for you know not what evil may happen on earth.
[3] If the clouds are full of rain,
they empty themselves on the earth;
and if a tree falls to the south or to the north,
in the place where the tree falls, there it will lie.
[4] He who observes the wind will not sow;
and he who regards the clouds will not reap.

[5] As you do not know how the spirit comes to the bones
in the womb of a woman with child, so you do not know
the work of God who makes everything.
[6] In the morning sow your seed, and at evening with-
hold not your hand; for you do not know which will
prosper, this or that, or whether both alike will be good.

Let go. Mystery is built in. Creation has patterns we cannot fathom, and that is good. Not knowing is not a state of affairs to be overcome, but a reality built into our lives. Koheleth has come a long way to get to this point.

Chapter 12 will bring a funereal goodbye. Last words from Koheleth. We have discussed the text above.

This is the lead-in to them:

> 7 Light is sweet, and it is pleasant for the eyes to behold
> the sun.
> 8 For if a man lives many years, let him rejoice in them
> all; but let him remember that the days of darkness will
> be many. [All that comes is beyond control.]
> 9 Rejoice, O young man, in your youth, and let your
> heart cheer you in the days of your youth; walk in the
> ways of your heart and the sight of your eyes. But know
> that for all these things God will bring you into judgment.
> 10 Remove vexation from your mind, and put away
> pain from your body; for youth and the dawn of life are
> *hebel*. [They are for their time. Not forever.]

When the funereal goodbye is completed, we have the epilogue. It commends Koheleth. The theme of final judgment is not foreign to the body of the work. And we have just heard it repeated. With it the book draws to a close.

We have heard the beginning and ending of wisdom. All has been heard. Beware of anything more. The grammar of strong and weak verbs and the most difficult constructions—all has now been set forth. God has the last word.

And thus the book concludes.

> Fear God and keep his commandments; for this is the whole duty of man. God will bring every deed into judgment, with every secret thing, whether good or evil.

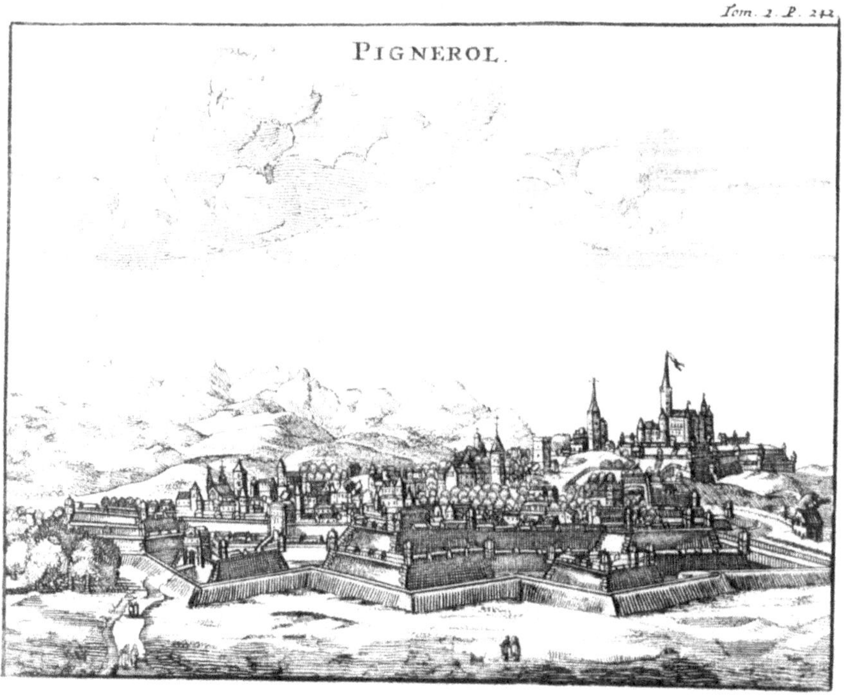

Pignerol cityscape, copper plate engraving, 1750.
Paris, Bibliothèque Nationale. Photo: akg-images.

5
Quo non Descendet?

Fouquet was being warned that his great successes would not necessarily mean great adulation. His character was optimistic and generous, and he was overlong in realizing the difficult place he was putting himself in. He began to carefully recruit networks of spies to keep him informed, and would shortly have to think seriously about plans for a possible ambush of his impressively powerful station. "For his part Nicolas realized that now he had to be especially careful. He had become too visible, too prosperous, too powerful not to be challenged."[1]

He is called to the provinces for a meeting with the Sun King. The latter has been very careful to avoid intimating anything resembling lack of trust in his Superintendent of Finances and attorney-general of the Parlement, Nicolas Fouquet. To be sure, his extremely close relationship with the king's mother Anne seems to have cooled. And with the death of Cardinal Mazarin there needs to be some overhaul of the way the kingdom has been managed. Jean-Baptiste Colbert,[2] who will prove in time to be the shrewd architect of his downfall, has moderated his relationship toward him in more congenial

[1] Charles Drazin, *The Man Who Outshone the Sun King: Ambition, Triumph and Treachery in the Reign of Louis XIV* (Random House, 2009), 178.

[2] For a blunt and brisk account showing the darkness of Colbert, see, among others, Paul Morand, *Fouquet, ou le soleil offusqué* (Gallimard, 1961), 152–53.

ways. The king did not bring Colbert into a position of greater authority but made him answerable to Fouquet—but only for a season. He will ultimately place himself in greater authority vis-à-vis the finances of France.

For our purposes, it is important to note how completely stunned Nicolas is when suddenly accosted by the captain-lieutenant of the musketeers, d'Artagnan: "I arrest you by order of the King." His calm response is, "But Monsieur d'Artagnan, are you sure it's *me* you're looking for?"

The scene is worth recounting.

"Nicolas got out of the litter and read the order of arrest. Determined to keep his self-composure, he allowed d'Artagnan to search him for papers. Sighing he said, 'I used to think the King held me in greater regard than anyone else in his kingdom.'"[3] Fouquet's motto, on view throughout Vaux-le-Vicomte the fateful night the king and his court, along with Jean-Baptiste Colbert, came to dinner, or *Quo ne Ascendet?* (To where will he not ascend?)—had its rude and definitive answer.

The trial lasted three years, during which time Fouquet nearly lost his life through illness and anxiety. He was exiled to the castle of Anjou under the supervision of the famous d'Artagnan, who would watch over him there and throughout this period, including at the Bastille in Paris. His wife and family were likewise banished to Limoges. "When he had been arrested at the beginning of the autumn, his hair was brown; but now, at the end of the year it was completely white."[4] The young son born at Fontainebleau would not see him again until many years later at Pignerol. His teeth were falling out, and he was a very beaten-down physical specimen.

We shall make note of his mother at this juncture. She had always worried about his spiritual health amid the trappings of wealth and the vanities of the world. Her life was of constant service to the poor and the sick. When her son gave her residence at the chateau of Saint-Mandé, filled with huge

3 Drazin, *Sun King*, 233.

4 Drazin, *Sun King*, 247.

stores of valuable goods beyond measure (one of the first places raided by Colbert, much of those goods now in the Louvre) she preferred a single bed and stand, a crucifix on the wall.

His chaplain, Père Deschamps-Neufs, was in charge of cataloging this increasingly voluminous collection of treasures. For his part, he was writing a commentary on the Psalms entitled *Les Soupirs de David* (The Sighs of David).[5] The work was dedicated to Fouquet. It was a not very subtle exhortation to his friend about where he should be placing his energies: in the Psalms and not in the vain pleasures of the world. As a biographer wryly noted, Fouquet handed the volume back to him to catalog and then file away.[6]

His many friends followed the trial closely, and their only relief was that the king's wish for hanging was stayed by a majority of the judges. But he would not be banished. He would be imprisoned for life.

There was one solitary figure, his mother, who watched things at a different plane of spiritual, not worldly, perception. When she learned of the arrest of her son, she dropped to her knees. "I thank you, my Lord. I have always begged you to save him. Here is the way." This was the fall of 1661.[7]

Three years later the final phase of the trial would unfold on November 14, 1664. Fouquet was so ill that only one hour a day could be given for him to be questioned and to respond. In one of those dramatic scenes that came alongside the years and years of her devoted care of the sick—Madame Fouquet was renowned for her medicinal treatments—a remarkable event took place before her son's final verdict.

The king's wife, Queen Maria Theresa, was gravely ill after giving birth to a premature child. A special day of prayer was held just before the trial was to be completed. Among

[5] "A Hebrew scholar of considerable repute, he spent much of his time working on translations of the Scriptures, but theoretically was on call for Nicolas to consult on spiritual matters whenever he felt the need" (Drazin, *Sun King*, 37).

[6] Drazin, *Sun King*, 188.

[7] Drazin, *Sun King*, 240.

the supplicants for the royal day of prayer was the Marquise de Charost, the daughter of Fouquet by his first wife.

> Finding the King's mother, Queen Anne of Austria, she gave her a special medicinal plaster that Nicolas's mother Marie had concocted for women after childbirth. The Queen Mother then took the plaster to Maria Theresa. "I'll put it on," she declared. "Madame Fouquet is a saint." The effect of the plaster was dramatic: two huge blood clots were worked loose from the Queen's insides, each one the side of a fist. In the corridors of the Louvre, people were saying that Madame Fouquet had worked a miracle.[8]

The queen mother quickly announced the miraculous news to her son the king. He refused to listen. His wife and his mother threw themselves at his feet, begging that mercy be shown to Nicolas. He ignored them.

On the day the verdict was to be announced the fear of Fouquet's friends and associates was that he be executed, which was the will of Louis XIV. Fouquet had now been under arrest and in the custody of d'Artagnan for more than three years, moving from prison to prison and finally to the Bastille. The biographer Jean-Christian Petitfils offers this account:

> Le lendemain à huit heures du matin, à la Bastille, d'Artagnan, curieux d'observer le comportement de son prisonnier, ouvre la porte sans bruit. Il le trouve au coin du feu, un livre de dévotion à la main, dans la quietude des jours precédents. Comme il s'étonne le voir si peu affairé, sans plume ni papier, celui-ci répond: "Je suis valet à louer, je n'ai plus rien a faire qu'à prier Dieu et à attendre le jugement. Quel qu'il soit, je le receverai avec la meme tranquillité d'esprit. Je suis résolu et préparé à tout."[9]

[8] Drazin, *Sun King*, 267.

[9] Jean-Christian Petitfils, *Fouquet* (Perrin, 1998), 441.

> The next day at eight o'clock in the morning, at the Bastille, d'Artagnan, curious to observe the behavior of his prisoner, opens the door without a sound. He finds him by the fire, a devotional book in hand, in the tranquility of previous days. As he is surprised to see him so idle, without pen or paper, he replies: "I am a valet for hire, I have nothing left to do but pray to God and wait for judgment. Whatever it is, I will receive it with the same peace of mind. I am resolute and prepared for anything."

The initial sentence was for banishment. A huge blow for the ever-scheming Colbert. The king himself was furious. The judges were confronted. The final sentence would end up being not death, nor banishment, but life imprisonment. Fouquet's family members were removed to the provinces. They were overjoyed that he had not been sentenced to death. On December 22, less than three hours after the verdict, in the dead of winter, Fouquet would begin the arduous three-week journey to Pignerol with a hundred musketeers riding alongside. The kindly, humane d'Artagnan allowed Fouquet to say goodbye to his household servant. He was strong and resolute. Those virtues would now be put to the severest test.

In this description I have wanted to set the stage for what will end up being an imprisonment of eighteen years' duration. Already one can see a dispossessed man, a saintly, miracle-working mother, and the beginning of a new kind of life altogether. Fouquet had been the wealthiest man in France, collector of art, antiquities, books, gardens, women, chateaux, grand relationships of importance throughout France. All that had come to an end.

The resemblances with the figure of Solomon in retrospective penitential mode are obvious enough, as well as the differences. Our point in this book is only to note distinctive realities within the same territory of dramatic descent from a great height. The protagonist of the book of Ecclesiastes has nothing like the same rich and detailed life story as the flesh-and-blood Fouquet. Fouquet is a man of modern historiographical recounting, and the sources for putting him before us are voluminous. Ecclesiastes and Fouquet are witnesses who speak at the end of their days, with testimonies to that final reality.

Furthermore, in the case of Ecclesiastes it is the reception history of the book that strongly reinforces a picture of penitential retrospection from a Solomon brought to his knees. We will need to examine the relationship between the canonical book and what it may allow us to infer, and a subsequent history of interpretation in Jewish and Christian circles that will close that gap.

The deportment of Fouquet after three years of ill health and constant imprisonment, awaiting his trial, gives us a glimpse of a man that we will now fast-forward so as to look at the final years of his life. For a major stretch of his time at Pignerol he was forbidden to write anything, and what we know of him comes from correspondence that we can now read (between Louvais the secretary for war and Saint-Mars), and the letters, bits of verse and spiritual reflection he was free to compose before his death. As noted, he believed he was about to be liberated, due to the increasingly lenient treatment he was receiving from Louis XIV, faithfully carried out by the governor jailor Saint-Mars.

Ecclesiastes occupies, then, something of the same space as *Les Conseils de la Sagesse.* Neither work is written by the men they purport to be about, but both stand in relationship to figures of history about which we can know more—"history" of course being of an altogether different character and genre for Solomon than for the seventeenth-century Superintendent of Finances. That does not prevent us from seeing important analogies at work in the way Ecclesiastes and *Les Conseils* bequeath a portrait to us. In the case of the latter, our "historical source material" is of a modern character, based upon contemporaneously written records.

What is of interest is the degree to which the portrayal of *Conseils* is in no small way consistent with, though different, to what we can say about a man whom the sources allow us more directly to see. The *Conseils* are reflections on the maxims of Solomon, and so have their own integrity in that form. But they come alongside the historical source material in complementary ways. We will turn to the writings that survive for us to inspect. In the following chapter I will look at the oblique authorial reference technique at work in both *Conseils* and Ecclesiastes. Though the works arise at very different points in time, to very different purposes, they also bear commonalities that warrant a look at them together.

We have an excellent view of Fouquet in prison precisely due to the obsessive character of statist absolutism. The correspondence running between the royal court and the royal jailor, Paris to the remote prison on the border of Savoie, is extensive. Here we learn of all the constraints, concerns, plots, intrigues animating the life of a royal fortress and its few but highly important clientele, including a man history will come to describe, with breathless and sustained interest, as wearing a *masque de fer.*

The conditions of his imprisonment were harsh. He was in a small and isolated cell. His valet was likely a spy, so conversation with him was of necessity guarded. A chaplain would arrive daily to say Mass, but as with the valet, the confessional was likely not confidential. If he asked for news, it was reported to Saint-Mars. The chaplain also warned the jailor about secret messages being written in the books loaned to the prisoner. Now confession was allowed only on major feasts, and all books were checked. Later this would extend to Fouquet's clothing and pieces of fabric and napkins, where he had written down things of importance to him. It is hard to imagine a lifetime of writing, so central to the exercise of his duties, now totally curtailed.

Though in isolation in the remote prison fortress miles from Paris, the general public there had not lost interest in him. A powder magazine insufficiently secured was struck by lightning at the prison. Over four hundred corpses of soldiers and workers were found in the rubble when the ruins were combed for survivors. Fouquet, his valet, and five soldiers were among the few survivors. When the news reached Paris, it was thought a miracle of God that the superintendent was spared. One poem begged Louis XIV to show leniency. "O, Louis, likeness of God, you in your turn imitate God supreme and pardon this poor man."[10] His response was to punish the poet.

Though he would feign disinterest and nonchalance about affairs surrounding the banished Fouquet, letters dispatched to Saint-Mars by Louvois indicate otherwise. One from 1666 reveals this was an outward appearance only. "Although His Majesty is entirely satisfied with the assurances you have given in your letters that Monsieur Fouquet is securely guarded, it would nonetheless be a good idea to give a few more details for particular satisfaction; he'd be very pleased if from time to time you'd describe the way in which the prisoner lives—whether he bears his captivity well or badly, what he says, and the things that happen in the course of his imprisonment."[11]

Fouquet was well supplied with reading materials, much of it devotional in character (Bonaventure was fine, no Augustine). His efforts to write on tablecloths and other schemes were thwarted. Once two supporters, including his servant La Forêt, to whom he had said goodbye on his way out of Paris, made their way to the place where he was staying and hailed him. They had bribed a guard. Astonished to see his old servant and a friend from Provence he recognized, he threw a written message from his window. The two were caught and summarily hung on orders of the king, along with the guards.

[10] Drazin, *Sun King*, 279.
[11] Drazin, *Sun King*, 281.

The appeal to the king to act like the True King, the Sovereign God, again showed no evidence of success. Shutters were installed on Fouquet's windows.

Several years would pass, and any hope for a change in his fate receded. His health was frequently quite poor. He was allowed to concoct the kinds of medications his mother had made famous and which he recalled with the help of his valet. In 1672, we learn, he was allowed to receive a message from his wife and respond, a full eight years after the trial verdict and their separation. Paper was brought, and he was permitted to write in his own hand, after some time for thought. A year later he persuaded Louvois to allow him to draw up some proposals to aid the king in a situation of financial challenge due to the war with the Dutch. When the response came back, he had been rebuffed. The letter was read to him and then burned in his presence.

We are entering the period of his long imprisonment where the evidence of his writings begins to emerge. This is against the backdrop of greater leniency, now that he had been in captivity for a decade. One senses a Fouquet coming onto a higher plane of spiritual insight and conviction. His illnesses and his isolation over so many years, and his loss of hope in any royal leniency, moved him to distinguish his obedience and loyalty to the earthly king, once called Donné de Dieu ("Given by God") and God the King Eternal.

Here is one of his penitential compositions.

Trompeuses vanités où mon âme abuseé
A vu de ses beaux jours la trame mal usée,
Esclavage de cour, où tous les courtisans
Dissipent en fumeé et leurs biens et leurs ans,
Vous ne me tenez plus: vos faux biens, vos faux charmes
Sont ici maintenant le sujet de mes larmes:
Je déplore le temps que j'ai perdu pour vous.
Vos favoris, vos rois qu'on adore à genoux
Au-dessus du commun n'ont qu'un éclat de verre

Ils sont faits comme nous de poussière et de terre.
Quand l'heure sonnera, malgré tous leurs efforts,
Leur pourpre et leur grandeur, leur trône et leurs
trésors,
Leur haute majesté tomberont dans la bière
Et quelques jours après ne sera que poussière![12]

Deceptive vanities! my abused soul
Has seen the ill-used frame of its good days.
The slavery of the court, where all courtiers
Dissipate in smoke; so too their goods and their years.
You no longer hold me: your false goods, your false
charms
Now are the subject of my tears.
I regret the time I lost for you:
Your favorites, your kings that we adore on our knees
Above the common are but a shard of glass.
They are made like us of dust and earth.
When the hour comes, despite all their efforts
Their property and their grandeur, their throne and
their treasures,
Their high majesty will fall into the casket.
And a few days later there will be nothing but dust.

In Chatelain's biography of Fouquet he writes, capturing the mind of the superintendent, "A demon had seduced the superintendent, the court had abused him, retirement in the bosom of God provided him with all true benefits."[13]

This from Fouquet's pen, the first line reminiscent of the tenth verse of Psalm 84.

Un seul jour avec Dieu vaut mieux que mille jours
Passes avec vos rois dans vos superbes cours;
Un mot, un contre-temps, une mauvaise œillade

[12] Petitfils, *Fouquet*, 478.

[13] Urbain-Victor Chatelain, *Le Surintendant Nicolas Foucquet, protecteur des lettres des arts et des sciences* (Perrin, 1905), 546.

Est capable de rendre un courtisan malade.
S'il faut prier le roi, s'il faut l'entretenir,
Il faut aller cent fois et cent fois revenir.
Parler au favori, faire cent révérences,
Payer avant qu'avoir de faibles récompensés:
Il n'en est pas ainsi du Dieu que nous servons.
Nous demandons sans cesse et toujours nous avons;
Toujours prêt d'écouter nos vœux et nos demandes
Plus nos désirs sont forts, plus ses grâces sont grandes.[14]

One day with God is better than a thousand days
Passed with your kings in your superb courts;
A word, a setback, a bad glance
Is capable of rendering ill to a courtier.
If we must pray to the king, if we must entertain him,
You have to go a hundred times and come back a
hundred times.
Speak to the favorite, make a hundred reverences,
Pay before having meager rewards:
This is not the case with the God we serve.
We always ask and always we have;
Always ready to listen to our wishes and requests.
The stronger our desires, the greater his graces.

"Such were the edifying compositions with which the superintendent occupied himself," Chatelain comments.[15]

Among the biographers of Fouquet chronicling this particular phase of his life (Chatelain, Dessert, Petitfils, Morand), it is Drazin who mentions Fouquet's early classical education at College de Clermont now being brought into service in the translating of the Psalms. "Once he had put his entire faith in the King, but now he thought of the King as an imposter."[16]

[14] As reproduced by Chatelain, *Foucquet*, 546.
[15] Chatelain, *Foucquet*, 546.
[16] Drazin, *Sun King*, 289.

God alone, the God of Gods and the King alone of
  kings
Deserves our care, devotion and labour:
To him alone do we owe our duty.
Anything given elsewhere is a theft and a crime.
So it is to this king, the King, that we must give our
  hearts,
Adoring him and serving him day and night.

The first effort at psalm translation we have notice of is, unsurprisingly, Psalm 118. He writes at the top of his page, "This psalm has considerable relevance to my present condition and to the eventual release that I hope for, God willing."[17] Anyone reading through this psalm will see lines "with considerable relevance."

When hard pressed, I cried to the Lord;
  he brought me into a spacious place.
The Lord is with me; I will not be afraid.
  What can mere mortals do to me?
The Lord is with me; he is my helper.
  I look in triumph on my enemies.

It is better to take refuge in the Lord
  than to trust in humans.
It is better to take refuge in the Lord
  than to trust in princes.

I will not die but live,
  and will proclaim what the Lord has done.
The Lord has chastened me severely,
  but he has not given me over to death.

[17] Drazin, *Sun King*, 290.

We are now in the latter half of the 1670s. The king has indeed begun to show greater clemency to Fouquet, and so his hope for release is not unreasonable. Louis XIV will eventually allow his wife and children to come visit him in 1679. His aging mother is too weak to make the journey. His hope for an end to his imprisonment will come as he has begun to place his trust completely in God. His former life of accumulation he looks back on in penitence. His letters to his mother are especially moving.[18] He speaks of kneeling before her and, through his tears, begging her forgiveness for the cares and stress he caused her through his life of dissolution. We are speaking about a man reborn into a living and eternal hope.

The attentive reader might at this point recall that, also at this time, a volume is published in Paris in 1677 called *Les Conseils de la Sagesse*. Biographers noting the congruence between his penitential writings—especially his concern to honor God the true King—and the contents of *Conseils* will at this juncture need to account for its place in the Fouquet biography. This will be the subject of the next chapter.

Suffice it to say here, the publication of a major work that situates the author in a place of solitude and reflection is intriguing on a number of different levels. The obvious thing is that the public will invariably draw the conclusion that here we are reading the compositions of the exiled Nicolas Fouquet. And so this happens. It is a view that persists in robust and indeed expanded form in the English translation we examined above, and those like it in other languages. And it is a view never seriously called into doubt until well into the nineteenth century, and even then, with those who reject this view or,

[18] "Kneeling before you, my heart, my mouth and perhaps my eyes, through their tears, will explain in depth what you now read in these few words, namely my intense sorrow for the pain that my wrong conduct has caused, disturbing the repose of your honest retirement, and taxing your goodness. Kneeling before you, I shall humbly beg your forgiveness for having made such a poor work of your good counsels and taken a path entirely contrary to your good example" (quoted from Drazin, *Sun King*, 300).

minimally, who question the attribution that is made with a little-known Michel Boutauld S.J.

That his known dates make Boutauld a ten-year-older contemporary of Fouquet, writing in 1677, three years before Fouquet's death and hoped-for release, means that even if we can credit him with the *Counsels of Wisdom* we are left asking why this book appeared and what was the motivation for its publication and release at this critical time in the life of the imprisoned Nicolas Fouquet.[19]

For now we are content to observe the true state of mind of Fouquet, and the writings that present to us the penitent and now liberated soul of a man truly free, no matter what the conditions of his captivity. He dies in prison, after eighteen years in custody, in 1680.

Something of his last words written provides a fitting tribute. He is writing his wife, whom he hopes will be able to visit him.

> For three months I have been waiting patiently to receive your letter. Now it has finally arrived and afforded me as much solace as I can feel in a place of such bitterness and pain. Nothing moves me so much as the cares you have taken over our chapel and the devotions you make there. For a long time now I have begged Saint-Mars and the priest who comes here to take my confession and allow me to prepare for my death—which I sense is not far off now—by allowing me free access to a good cleric who is above suspicion, to whom I can open up my conscience without reserve concerning the bad life I have led, to give me instruction . . . to strengthen me by the ordinary aids that God has instituted for the life and nourishment of Christian souls, and finally to offer consolation for my continual displeasure and to warm my too often sullen *froideur*. . . . I look at the letter from my mother as both a miracle and a sort of holy relic. Her hand

[19] See appendix 1 below.

> is stronger than mine, and her goodness surpassing for a son who has given her so much unhappiness. Continue and redouble your supplications to God and to those exercising his authority on earth, so that you might come and spend some time here and gain the freedom to see me . . . There is nothing against reason or against justice that after fourteen years of absence a woman might see her husband in the decline of his life, and I hope that a glorious monarch, one whom God makes triumphant over all Europe, will find it appropriate, for the love and in honor of the same God, to pardon and grant some small relief to one of his subjects whose person, good, and hope are in his power. If I behaved badly, I was punished, and I had time to do penance.
>
> I praise God that, as you indicate, our children are in a good disposition, each according to their age. It is of his singular benediction that the sins of a father are not left to harm the family of so virtuous a mother. Nurture well what is good in them and endeavor to turn them from vice and from embracing frivolity, which is a pernicious inclination of many in our family. Instill in their hearts a firmness of gratitude toward those from whom they receive good will, and careful attention to watch their speech. That and the fear of God will above all see to their prosperity.
>
> Finally, what is most sure now is leaving cares for the body behind, and thinking of the soul. Give my regards to my brothers and sisters, should they still be alive.
>
> Please embrace for me my daughter and commend me to the prayers of your community.[20]

"Nicolas here reveals to us the modesty, the wisdom, and the depth of a soul steeped in the word of God. How he has changed! Humility has killed in him the last tumults of the

[20] My translation of the letter as reproduced in its entirety by Petitfils, *Fouquet*, 478–80.

world. This letter was copied and sent forth into the circle of his relatives and friends, who have never let its memory fade."[21]

As it was, in the mercy and kindness of God Fouquet would live just long enough to see his family again. In June of 1679, "Nicolas, tears in his eyes, pressed in his arms the members of his dear family: his wife, forced to part from him at 30 years old, pretty and charming, whom he receives now in her early fifties, gray-haired and her face wrinkled," his brother with wife, his eldest son, daughter, and youngest son.[22] He would die in less than a year, in the company of the family he had prayed to God to let him see again.

[21] Petitfils, *Fouquet*, 480.
[22] Petitfils, *Fouquet*, 491.

6
Whither Wisdom?

In this chapter I leave the discussion of Fouquet, *Counsels*, and authorship, and reenter the standard scholarly world in which Ecclesiastes interpretation has followed certain general trends. These are now under negotiation. Getting the proper angle of vision on how Ecclesiastes is meant to function in relationship to King Solomon, and where it sits more loosely to that connection, has been discussed using the example of Fouquet and the *Conseils*. Here we look at it in context of the classic world of modern study of Israel's "wisdom literature." Let's begin with a resonant passage from the book of Job:

> **28** [1] There is a mine for silver
> and a place where gold is refined.
> [2] Iron is taken from the earth,
> and copper is smelted from ore.
> [3] Mortals put an end to the darkness;
> they search out the farthest recesses
> for ore in the blackest darkness.
> [4] Far from human dwellings they cut a shaft,
> in places untouched by human feet;
> far from other people they dangle and sway.
> [5] The earth, from which food comes,
> is transformed below as by fire;
> [6] lapis lazuli comes from its rocks,
> and its dust contains nuggets of gold.

7 No bird of prey knows that hidden path,
no falcon's eye has seen it.
8 Proud beasts do not set foot on it,
and no lion prowls there.
9 People assault the flinty rock with their hands
and lay bare the roots of the mountains.
10 They tunnel through the rock;
their eyes see all its treasures.
11 They search the sources of the rivers
and bring hidden things to light.
12 But where can wisdom be found?
Where does understanding dwell? (NIV)

Job asks where wisdom comes from. Where it can be found. One can open a mine shaft and drill deep into the bowels of the earth, laying bare treasures and precious stones all the more valuable because so hidden and hard to extract. But wisdom is harder to find.

One could say the same thing about the use of the term *wisdom* in biblical studies. Does it refer to an idea, a school, a profession (sages joining prophets and priests), a movement, a genre, or perhaps a distinct body of literature, to be called Wisdom Literature? This would make the quest far simpler, one supposes. We have prophetic books and we have Torah. Can we not also speak then of wisdom literature? Proverbs, Job, and Ecclesiastes have been regular candidates for this category, joined at times for scholarly treatments by the Greek books Sirach and Wisdom of Solomon.

One does not need to drill deep down into the earth to find this "wisdom literature." There it is. All one must do is put the books in some kind of sequence.

A popular one is Proverbs–Job–Ecclesiastes. Proverbs represents a coherent, even unified school of wisdom centered on the pithy maxim. The book of Job starts with this standard premise, but we then watch it come apart. Ecclesiastes does not bother to even start there. It is a literature of pessimism about any kind of (natural or school-based) wisdom. It cannot be found. The quest for it is doomed. Job, in retrospect, should have known that from the beginning. We can call this the wisdom journey: starts out promising and ends in failure. Do not read Proverbs. It is simplistic and wrong.[1]

We are of course running past some obvious problems. There is no canonical category for something to be called "wisdom literature." Here the contrast with Torah and Prophets is obvious. We have a Pentateuch carefully marked as five books. We have a Prophetic division of the canon, Former and Latter, and the subdivision of the second category is as familiar as are the five books of Moses: Three Major Prophets and the Book of the Twelve.

One may ask why there are two divisions and why the first one, running from Joshua to 2 Kings, seems distinctive. Or why Daniel arrives to find its place from time to time. But that is a simple question to answer compared with the invention of a tidy category called "wisdom literature" which nowhere has any comparable canonical marking. These books are found in the miscellany or library section of the Hebrew canon, and they never appear in that order. Rather, we have two kindred sequences focused on the figure of Solomon, either Proverbs–Ecclesiastes–Song of Songs (note we have said nothing of that book thus far) or Proverbs–Song of Songs–Ecclesiastes. Job is one of the big books usually placed alongside the Psalms. Its hero is not an Israelite but a predecessor of Noah, and the friends who come to comfort him are likewise antediluvian foreigners. Indeed, part of the dilemma the book so keenly places before us—Can a mortal serve God

[1] See the brief discussions in Christopher R. Seitz, "A Canonical Reading of Ecclesiastes," in *Acts of Interpretation: Scripture, Theology, and Culture*, ed. S. A. Cummins and Jens Zimmerman (Eerdmans, 2018); and *The Heights of the Hills Are His Also* (Baylor University Press, 2024), vii–xi. The reading of Job proposed here is laid out in the second half of *Heights* (55–99). A recent rejection of the "wisdom literature" classification is Will Kynes, *An Obituary for "Wisdom Literature": The Birth, Death, and Intertextual Reintegration of a Biblical Corpus* (Oxford University Press, 2019).

for nought?—makes its most poignant sense when this pre-Torah, generalizable challenge is kept in just that context. As Luther said, the patriarchs must face God in his *Urgewalt.* El Shaddai.

The only way to get Job to range alongside Proverbs and Ecclesiastes is to theorize a "wisdom literature" category in which it represents a medial deconstructing phase. One needs a theory of historical—not canonical—context that tells us we have a residual folktale in which conservative proverbial wisdom is being pulled apart by friends waiting to enroll in the school of Ecclesiastes, a book contemporaneous with the dialogues of Job. But, of course, Job does not come to us in theoretical layers of development. The wisdom of the prologue is of a piece with the epilogue, which has the final word. Job's is a hard-fought but real wisdom.

I will come back to this point in a moment. The main thing to be noted is that we have no wisdom literature represented in the form in which it has become popularized when we look at the canonical presentation itself. "Wisdom literature" is part and parcel with the idea that the canonical orders are not significant, hermeneutically or theologically. But as that idea loses its grip on interpretation, so too does the invention of a category called "wisdom literature" along with dating schemes held to be of crucial interpretive importance. Nothing prevents a postexilic author from laying hold of an antediluvian hero like Job and making him the centerpiece of his theological masterpiece precisely as that same antediluvian hero, whose struggle is more intense and more meaningful on the terms the book gives it to us.

The most obvious thing to be noted in terms of canonical order is the triad of books mentioned above. The broadly Jewish view of the Solomonic books is that the sequence represents an aging process. Proverbs comes from the king's classical education, Songs from his libidinal heyday, and Ecclesiastes his old age and grey hair. This life journey is not a repudiation of first and second phases but a mature appreciation of them as death approaches. On one account, to which we will return, the author has lost his name and been given a new one, Koheleth, on account of his sins, as recorded in the last chapters associated with him in Kings. He was faithless, built idols, forgot the Lord. But the main point here is that Ecclesiastes shows us *a man who knows all this to be so*, and who is contrite in a manner that opens doors onto the deepest wisdom. In his loss of a name he is even further an Adam not far from each and every one of us.

The Christian tradition has worked with a slightly different but still allied idea of three books and a sequence. Proverbs and classical education: You learn the strong verbs first. You get the "driver's education" version suitable for beginning to get behind the wheel. Ecclesiastes is real wisdom: Exceptions to the rule. The weak verbs that in point of fact are different precisely because used more often, and so reflect long experience and malleability. Wisdom must negotiate the rule and the exception if it is to be wisdom, and having done that one breaks into Song. For the early church father Origen, here we have the language of heaven and eternity for which we must be made fit by a wisdom not gained but endowed from on high. Grasping that gives way to loss that gives way to a new kind of open hand.

One can see though that, with a different sequence, the same basic wisdom is being imparted, and this precisely as the books are read together and not transferred to a new kind of "wisdom literature" category where Song falls out and Job is misfitted in. There is a good reason for leaving that majestic book alone to do its majestic thing. In its canonical form it has its own journey we are asked to take alongside its hero, where we know things Job does not know and where that knowledge cannot impede the titanic struggle Job must undertake if Satan's wager is to be defeated. The brilliance of the canonical form is ruined if the book is chopped into threes (folktale, dialogues, divine speech/wisdom poem) so as to be placed inside the artificial framework of deteriorating wisdom. Immediately the genius of the form, in which Job and reader face different challenges under different conditions, comes under threat. Instead, we journey alongside our hero and watch him triumph through what the Epistle of James called the *hypomone* of Job: his perseverance, standing when others leave.

My intention in this chapter has been to clear the ground for a fresh look at Ecclesiastes, once we get the proper angle of vision from which to approach it. Here the "wisdom literature" idea has become a hindrance.

But it might be useful to stop and ask how the notion took hold in the first place. It is easy enough to speak of a descent in confidence in wisdom. "Go to the ant, thou sluggard" always has the potential for the observer to learn nothing or to pull out bug spray. That is built into the equation, and the fact is not lost on the book of Proverbs itself. Proverbs is not a monochromatic "a stitch in time saves nine" sort of collection. It consists of varieties of forms, and it contains tensions and seeming disagreements over what it commends. Does the wise young man hold his tongue or does the wise young man speak up? You can find both sentiments. Something more is needed than naked observation of the ways of the world. The fear of the Lord is the beginning of wisdom. Wisdom has a beginning, and it has an end. "The end of the matter, all has been heard. Fear God and keep his commandments." It does not have an all-comprehending middle, a porch swing of confident knowledge.

If one looks at the roots of the idea of a distinctive wisdom literature one will see the emphasis on Solomon prior to the mid-nineteenth century. Matters of historical authorship did not weigh so heavily. The Greek-language books of Sirach and Wisdom of Solomon already make any simple "Solomon holding the pen" idea inadequate. Gregory of Nyssa and all the early commentators made note of the failure to name Solomon by name in Ecclesiastes as worthy of reflection. On his account the lack of reference to Solomon was to prevent us reading the book as primarily autobiography. He wanted a larger dimension of significance to be available than such a categorization would allow. The point is that the Solomonic association, and the idea of a body of wisdom literature coalescing around it, was sufficiently flexible to accommodate the demanding subject matter that any evaluation of wisdom requires.

I have thus far been referring to a canonical arrangement, or presentation, that looks to an order going back to relatively consistent Hebrew tradition. Torah, Prophets, Writings. Modern English printed Bibles follow a different order in which the classical prophetic books come last, and the former prophets have been joined by historical books of like content from the Writings library. This has resulted in a fourfold order: Torah, Historical Books, Lyrical Books, and Prophets. The wise among you should note that in some ways I have made up the category "Lyrical Books," following others before me. What this category really is, is all the books left over when the more historical books (Chronicles, Ezra-Nehemiah, Esther) have been extracted, or those more topically akin to friendly neighbors (Daniel after Ezekiel; Lamentations after Jeremiah; Ruth after Judges). What remains after this exercise is a new division, if that is the right word for it: Psalms, Job, Proverbs, Ecclesiastes, Song of Songs.[2]

If one bothers to look at the lists that exist in Christian tradition (the Jewish is simpler) prior to the convention of our modern English Bibles, a few things are immediately obvious. (1) There is no fixed sequence but rather lots of different orders; no one seemed too exercised by this, and Jerome's wish for clarity and deference to the Hebrew Verity did not defeat either old habits or indifference about variety. (2) Malachi (final book of the Twelve Minor Prophets) is never last, though it

[2] For a fuller discussion see Christopher R. Seitz, *Elder Testament: Canon, Theology, Trinity* (Baylor University Press, 2018); as well as "The Canonical Function of the *Nebi'im*," in *Canon Formation: Tracing the Role of Sub-Collections in the Biblical Canon*, ed. W. Edward Glenny and Darien R. Lockett (T&T Clark, 2023), 167–81.

"leans into Matthew" and John the Baptist as Elijah to come. (3) Something like the Hebrew order, with books from the Writings in final position, often appears in vestigial form in Greek lists. The relative fixity of the Hebrew tripartite is not in evidence, but equally too the fourfold with which we are familiar is fully absent. What is preserved is the Solomonic triad in Hebrew and Greek. In modern orders, so too. But the one we are familiar with, with the Lyrical Book category, has them ranged behind with Job and Psalms.

A second reality needs to be considered alongside this. How to organize a curriculum for students? We can see reference to the curriculum in Divinity from the sixteenth century at the University of St Andrews. The Solomonic books were taught as a block if you happened to be studying in that fine school.

A modern curriculum for a seminary in which coverage of all the books of Old and New Testaments was a desired goal, a so-called survey course, has to make decisions about how to present the material and how best to distribute the lectures and readings. The entire NT being about a fifth the size of the OT means NT colleagues, as usual, don't have to work as hard as their Hebrew Bible counterparts. Historically oriented NT survey courses do Paul in semester one, Gospels and Acts in semester two, and work in Catholic Epistles and Revelation in some manner.

Old Testament survey courses deal with the Pentateuch in semester one. They figure out how to broker the complexities and irrelevancies of nineteenth-century theories of JEDP. They may ponder whether Deuteronomy belongs with the books that follow, or whether the Pentateuch is better thought of as a Hexateuch including Joshua. Or they may just glance at the idea and get on with the Torah first and Former Prophets second. Here we see something of a congenial coming-alongside of printed Bibles and classroom curriculum. Former Prophets are of course historical in character and different in kind from the classical prophets with which they are conjoined in the

Hebrew tradition. Both are called "Nebi'im" and are distinct from Torah and Writings. But in modern critical studies, the Former Prophets grouping comes nicely alongside the idea of a Deuteronomistic History. Deuteronomy as book one of a history beginning with a new generation entering the land (whose future disobedience is anticipated at the end of that same book) and ending—after first the separation of the Northern Kingdom and its demise—with the destruction of the temple, deportation to Babylon, and extinction of the monarchy.

So, Pentateuch and Deuteronomistic History in semester one. Creation to exile. Torah and Former Prophets corresponding to parts one and two of English printed Bibles, with Former Prophets representing a continuous historical record prior to the return from exile and restoration.

Semester two does not, however, pick up with the third division (Lyrical Books) but rather tackles the classical prophets. Typically, rather like the letters of Paul, these are not treated in the order we find them but instead according to a reconstructed chronological sequence. The second prophet Amos starts the sequence, followed by Hosea and Micah, with portions of Isaiah spliced in, Jeremiah, others of the Twelve, Ezekiel, Isaiah again, and ending with Jonah or Malachi. Publishing houses come into their own here, as introductions to the prophets (along these lines and as self-contained works) are easily packaged. Standard, historically oriented "Introductions to the Old Testament" also cover this territory reasonably well. So far, so good.

But notice what has been left out, given the attention to historical unfolding and reconstructions of proper sequence. Section three of English printed Bibles has become stranded. The lyrical books (Psalms, Job, Proverbs, Ecclesiastes, Song of Songs) just do not fit well in this standard operating procedure. Obviously, they are important books and so deserve their own proper treatment. So the genre "wisdom literature" was born and textbooks got generated. Another factor is also clear: These are not books that fit easily into the chronological, one-thing-after-another model that dominates in other parts of the standard introductions. Their proper interpretation does not turn on securing for them a historical context in the same way. Though scholars have tried, with the evolutionary model.

The basic outlines of this "textbook genre" go back to the mid-nineteenth century, unsurprisingly, given the field's investment in historical approaches as the sole key to proper interpretation. This material does not fit that model.

But another factor came into play due to the same historical impulse of the day. Questions were raised about whether and how Solomon might rightly be thought of as the author of the three books traditionally associated with him. Even the conservative flank represented by Franz Delitzsch famously said that if Koheleth is not postexilic, "there is no history of the Hebrew language." Technical study of the Hebrew language had evolved to a point where much of the vocabulary found in Ecclesiastes gave clear evidence of a much later date than Solomon and the wisdom famously associated with him in the narratives of 1 Kings, that is, the era of David and the founding of the monarchy.

A certain high seriousness accompanied this separation of Ecclesiastes from Solomon, forgetting of course that in the book itself the association is already at one step removed. The name Solomon never appears, even as some kind of association does seem intended. The earliest precritical commentators noted this and considered its significance exegetically, without all the high-flying concern for authorship and dating and history of the Hebrew language, as marked the nineteenth and twentieth centuries.

To summarize. One way of handling the wisdom books would have been to slot them alongside the contexts they themselves set forth. That is, treat the Solomonic trio when one is dealing with 1 Kings. There Solomon is the wise source of proverbial wisdom, the amorous king with enough wives to woo with Song of Songs-like wooing. And the king who fell off the rails later in life. Job, we are told in the book of Daniel, is a contemporary of the preflood patriarch Noah. This would help explain the book's strange aura. Its hero is pre-Israel and non-Israel, as are his friends. The divine name as revealed to Moses plays no role. Rather, we have the fearsome El Shaddai and a climate Luther described as one where God appears in his *Urgewalt*, his primordial, pre-Law majesty, darkness, and power.

It was above all the search for the proper historical location of an alleged author and audience that recalibrated the canonical context the books themselves ask us to read them in. Not Solomon—directly or more obliquely. Not David and the Psalter. Not Job and Noah. Rather, a postexilic situation of wisdom in crisis, for Ecclesiastes. Not a Job under trial on the terms the book presupposes, staring into the abyss of underserved suffering of a kind not restricted to the covenant people. A book needing to be understood as an attack on the pious moralism of the opening two chapters, the proverbial "Shall we not receive evil from the Lord, as well as the good?" A Psalter now detached from David because we cannot imagine him writing in the cave of Adullam (Ps 57). These canonical guidelines are removed as later modifications of the historical.

Thus far we have been holding up a different model for interpreting the book of Ecclesiastes. Our modest point here is that the "wisdom literature" genre emerged due to (1) certain reasons related to dating books as crucial to interpretation and (2) a failure to take seriously the canonical arrangements of books, in which wisdom has no genuine, single literary setting. The order of English printed Bibles, where Psalms, Job, Proverbs, Ecclesiastes, and Song of Songs are what remains when historical books have been removed from the Ketuvim (Writings), does not create any wisdom literature in the sense of popular textbook versions. The Solomonic emphasis is clear, and that is equally clear in the order of the Ketuvim.

The argument can be made that attention is now being paid to the final form of the Pentateuch (not just alleged sources), the Former Prophets as a coherent unit (represented by the so-called Deuteronomistic History), the Latter Prophets as Classical Prophecy in standard textbook form, and more recently to the order and significance of the Twelve Minor Prophets as we find them, and not recast in an "Amos to Jonah" historical model.

What is needed then is a better understanding of the character of the Writings, the third division of the canon. Instead of "wisdom literature" we have a collection of writings that are a miscellany, a library. Unlike the other divisions where order and sequence are significant indexes for interpretation, this division is not dependent on a specific arrangement of its parts for approaching its meaning. This would explain why the stability of ordering we note elsewhere gives way to three or four dominant patterns in the Writings.

I have argued that the reason for this is that the Writings are composed with reference to books outside their division. Job with Genesis. Psalms with David. Chronicles and Ezra-Nehemiah with Kings (Chronicles is in fact a "Genesis to Exile and Return reprise," "A to Z," book). Ruth with Judges. Lamentations with Jeremiah. Proverbs, Ecclesiastes, Song of Songs with Solomon. Law has a source in Moses. Praise in David. Wisdom in Solomon. In the postexilic period attention returns to the past, and Great Founders are seen as the source from which what we mean by law, praise, and wisdom arise. This is less a historical claim as a theological and hermeneutical one. To be a pray-er in the proper sense is to live in the spirit of David.

So, to the general question, Whither wisdom? one answer is: a fresh, careful, thoughtful appreciation of the canonical division of the Writings. Unfortunately, such work has been hindered at a number of points. One is the existence of a different order in most English printed Bibles, such that the very character of the third section is hard to evaluate as significant. A second is the consequence of an account of the development of the canon in which we are asked to think of successive phases of "closure"—Torah first, then Prophets, and finally the Writings. Fortunately, we are now far better poised to appreciate the way Torah and Prophets are mutually influencing in their formation and come to be what they are as different sections by collaboration, not by a "this first and that next" sequence. "Closure" has been a highly misleading idea, imported from conciliar decisions when it comes to the New Testament side of the question. There were no closure councils for the Hebrew Bible, and it is indeed possible to speak of canon without majoring in fixed orders, exact book number limits, and closure.

The Writings are not books left over when sections one and two in time stabilize. They are simply different in character. In theory, their total number could be one or two more or one or two less. They are independent works, and inside the division they can move and do. And in certain orderings to come they will even migrate outside of the third division to make the intended associative character with them more clear.

Here is a typical evaluation of the Writings, representative of a new model in which wisdom literature is being reconceived.

> The third, Writings section, in which all of the so-called Wisdom books are found, appears to be a miscellany, as its name suggests, composed of books that are unified only in their idiosyncrasy: their defining feature being their lack of fit among either the Law or the Prophets.[3]

The Torah and Prophets divisions represent achievements of internal association. The books of the Ketuvim are not "later" and "subsequent" and so unable to "fit in"; some of them are manifestly earlier or contemporaneous with books in the other two divisions. The character of the Ketuvim is different, taken as a totality. The Writings—the name is surely accurate—are more independent of each other inside the Ketuvim and more organically related to books outside the division.

[3] Will Kynes, "Wisdom Literature: An Obituary," *JTS* 69 (2018): 4.

Even the loose association of the three Solomonic books with each other can take two different forms in Jewish and Christian reception. A third arrangement arrived later, grouping the five smallest books: Song of Songs and Ecclesiastes join Ruth, Lamentations, and Esther in the liturgical sequence of subsequent Jewish religious use, for Passover, Weeks, the Destruction of the Temple, Booths, and Purim.

To conclude. The Ketuvim is a distinctive division. In the history of interpretation we see the books capable of migration and reordering, in a way that marks them over against the Torah and Prophets. That is consistent with their associative and miscellaneous character. Good treatments of the Writings will not focus on an "original" order and demand attention to it against alternatives, but rather will attend to how the differences are explicable and hermeneutically thoughtful rearrangements. Proverbs 31 asks, "Who is the woman of valor?" and Boaz answers, "Ruth." Judges shows us what life is like before the calling of David the son of Jesse, and Ruth promises that all is under God's providential care, anticipating the song of Hannah in 1 Samuel.

If the Writings are allowed to function as their own distinctive division, the recourse to a model popularizing the "wisdom literature"—one now under fire—will be replaced by a different set of considerations. The Solomonic trio will reemerge as canonically significant, and not on the terms of the "defensive authorship" argument.

7
Authorship, Inspiration, Reception
Hermeneutical Observations

The Reformation is typically credited with focusing the church's attention on the literal sense of Scripture, as against the spiritual senses of allergy, tropology, and other interpretive concerns. Childs, among others, has shown that concern with the *sensus literalis* and how it is to be understood was always at the forefront of scriptural interpretation in every era.[1] What becomes true in time is the way in which the literal sense is made to function in the domain of historical reference as its chief logical sphere. The literal sense is also closely allied with theories of authorial intention. Luther could use "Moses" as a shorthand for what he regarded as the literal-sense intention of the first five books of the Bible, and Calvin operated in similar vein. For both, the literal sense's pressure on the faithful church was due to God's inspiring of agents doing his bidding, prophets and apostles.

To ask about the historical location of the human author and the audience being addressed in the past would be for the Reformers something other than a concern for the divinely inspired literal sense. Removing the "clutter" of higher senses no longer attached to the literal or plain sense did not translate

[1] Brevard S. Childs, "The *Sensus Literalis* of Scripture: An Ancient and Modern Problem," in *Beiträge zur alttestamentlichen Theologie: Festschrift für Walther Zimmerli zum 70. Geburtstag*, ed. Herbert Donner, Robert Hanhart, and Rudolph Smend (Vandenhoeck & Ruprecht, 1977), 80–93.

into a search for facts in history not immediately brokered and foregrounded by the final form of the text as it does its communicative work. "Sources" of the Pentateuch, as a way to speak about the literal sense, would not have been in their purview. The distance, then, between a medieval interpreter like Aquinas, who prioritized the literal sense while recognizing the divine author's range in other ways, and Calvin and Luther is minimal. Due to the Scripture's two-testamental character, the Old Testament authors both speak intelligibly to communities in time and, being inspired, say more than could be contained by any historical intention we might recover by purely naturalist hermeneutics and archeology.

The shift to preoccupation with the "intention of the historical author"—away from the earlier concern for allowing the literal-sense scope to speak clearly—marks the intellectual trends emerging in the eighteenth century and the rise of natural and historical sciences.

In the case of a book like Ecclesiastes, this creates some very odd discussions and debates. The same is true in a whole host of places. This is because the way a biblical book presents its "author" is very different than might be assumed in a quest for a human author in time having a single intention. Indeed, to use a word like "author" against the backdrop of modernity, and book publishing, is to introduce a frame of reference foreign to the Scriptures of Old and New Testament. Even relatively clear cases, like the letters of Paul to congregations, upon inspection of just those letters leave only shards in our hands. Paul dictated letters, was not a professional scribe, and likely would have been unbothered by editing not directly his own, so long as it conformed with the larger tenor of his "intentions." This is not the place to get bogged down. My point is simply that with "Isaiah," "Joel," "Job," "Deuteronomy," and myriad biblical examples, the historical human author recedes just to the degree that the literary sense assembles itself in the form we have it—in contemporary parlance, its "canonical form and shape."

In the nineteenth century particularly, armed with the high priority being placed on "authorial intention" for hermeneutics, we get decades of detailed debates over the authorship of Isaiah (a sixty-six chapter composition), all of the Minor Prophets, the so-called wisdom books, and in the case of the Pentateuch a tidal wave of theories about how its composition is to be reconfigured in terms of sources, forms, traditions, redactions, subsequent editing, and so forth. When one turns to the Synoptic Gospels, the clutch having been released there as well, the situation is even more complicated, if that is possible. If there are more than three hundred theories of how the Gospels came to be, one might say the wrong questions are being put to the text, along the lines of the inherited "human author intention" model.

Armed with a clearer understanding of the history of the Hebrew language, a rough profile of the diachronic dimensions of an individual biblical book came into greater focus. The Hebrew of Ecclesiastes did not line up with the Hebrew of the period of the monarchy. But equally in that book's case, or Job's where the same indexes would be invoked, why might anyone think that Solomon "wrote" Ecclesiastes in the first place? One is tempted to say that the wrong toolbox has been brought out to start to do the work required.

Here we might ask ourselves whether the legitimate earlier concerns with prioritizing the literal sense are not in fact correct, insofar as they work along the grain with the final form of a work and are not seeking some form of historicity hidden behind it. The "canonical sense" attunes itself to evaluating the final form. Where it differs from earlier concern for the literal sense is the historical moment in time in which it works. It is prepared to acknowledge that the coming-to-be of a book is a factor in why the book looks like it does in its final form. It can even make judgments about what editors and shapers of received traditions have chosen to foreground and leave more obscure. But it does this in the name not of excavating the obscurities but respecting why they are as they are, and why the literal sense makes clear what it seeks to prioritize.

Ecclesiastes and Solomon

Let us put this notice from 1 Kings 11 in the record for our orientation in what follows.

> 1 Now King Solomon loved many foreign women:
> the daughter of Pharaoh, and Moabite, Ammonite,
> Edomite, Sidonian, and Hittite women, 2 from the
> nations concerning which the Lord had said to the
> people of Israel, "You shall not enter into marriage
> with them, neither shall they with you, for surely they
> will turn away your heart after their gods"; Solomon
> clung to these in love. 3 He had seven hundred wives,
> princesses, and three hundred concubines; and his wives
> turned away his heart. 4 For when Solomon was old
> his wives turned away his heart after other gods; and
> his heart was not wholly true to the Lord his God, as
> was the heart of David his father. 5 For Solomon went
> after Ashtoreth the goddess of the Sidonians, and after
> Milcom the abomination of the Ammonites. 6 So Solo-
> mon did what was evil in the sight of the Lord, and
> did not wholly follow the Lord, as David his father had
> done. 7 Then Solomon built a high place for Chemosh
> the abomination of Moab, and for Molech the abom-
> ination of the Ammonites, on the mountain east of
> Jerusalem. 8 And so he did for all his foreign wives, who
> burned incense and sacrificed to their gods.
>
> 9 And the Lord was angry with Solomon, because
> his heart had turned away from the Lord, the God
> of Israel, who had appeared to him twice, 10 and had
> commanded him concerning this thing, that he should
> not go after other gods; but he did not keep what
> the Lord commanded. 11 Therefore the Lord said to
> Solomon, "Since this has been your mind and you have
> not kept my covenant and my statutes which I have
> commanded you, I will surely tear the kingdom from

> you and will give it to your servant. [12] Yet for the sake
> of David your father I will not do it in your days, but
> I will tear it out of the hand of your son. [13] However I
> will not tear away all the kingdom; but I will give one
> tribe to your son, for the sake of David my servant and
> for the sake of Jerusalem which I have chosen."

A very useful essay shows itself under the compact title "Solomon and Qoheleth."[2] It is a study of the relationship between the figure of King Solomon and the book of Ecclesiastes (with attention also to Song of Songs and Proverbs, for contrast). Incidentally, it is a useful shorthand resource for Ecclesiastes in Jewish and Christian reception history. (The major comprehensive volume dedicated to this can be found in the Blackwell commentary series, by Eric Christianson.[3]) Weeks's essay charts a different course since the subsequent history of interpretation is rehearsed so as to show its distorting and misinterpreting tendencies. Sometimes this is done humorously and otherwise with studied seriousness. So, about the *Conseils* he remarks, "This is itself another illustration of interpretation shaping an account of Solomon, unusually turning him into a suburban commuter."[4] That is, the standard interpretative model is raised up to show how it has fumbled the ball. The main goal is to free interpretation of Ecclesiastes from association with Solomon.

In Weeks's model, the book of Ecclesiastes (and Scripture in general) is like an artefact. There is a pure isotope called "the book of Ecclesiastes." It really has nothing to do with Solomon (he uses interchangeably the terms "authorship" and "attribution"). "Countless commentators across the centuries have sought to align Ecclesiastes with the life of Solomon,

[2] Stuart Weeks, "Solomon and Qoheleth," in *Megilloth Studies: The Shape of Contemporary Scholarship*, ed. Brad Embry, Hebrew Bible Monographs 78 (Sheffield Phoenix, 2016), 71–86.

[3] Eric Christianson, *Ecclesiastes Through the Centuries*, BBC (Wiley-Blackwell, 2008).

[4] Weeks, "Solomon and Qoheleth," 76.

and in particular take the description of Qoheleth's works in chapter 2 as a summary of Solomon's works."[5] Parenthetically, I am unclear why the book would even invoke Solomon at all in the opening chapters in a manner he regards as inconsequential ("The scope for this has proved rather limited.") Shouldn't the book just keep its distance consistently? Why would the book include such a piece of autobiography at all? That it means to invoke Solomon, in whatever way we understand it, seems obvious.

Weeks starts by citing the use of Ecclesiastes in the festival context (Feast of Booths) as derived from the five-scroll *Megilloth*, so as to say this subsequent use is curiosity or contrivance. The festivals use the shortest books of the Ketuvim; two suit their contexts and the others are chosen for their brevity. Whatever shared context—the transitoriness of life—that might be said to exist between the Feast of Booths and Ecclesiastes plays no essential role. Weeks can describe Ecclesiastes as a book that "seems to commend piety and the fear of God . . . and to portray itself as the work of a man late in life, who looks back on his accomplishments, and who admonishes the young," but then finds no basis for this view of Solomon in the narrative tradition. Solomon's latest years, according to Weeks, show him at his "most worldly and least God-fearing."[6] To my mind at least, we can again see an effort to maintain something like two distinctive isotopes, one Solomon, one Ecclesiastes, as if one could not see in 1 Kings 11 any space at all for a king now come under the judgment of God, with all that might suggest about his state of mind, and the scope to say more about that.

Next are the Jewish and Christian stories of Solomon that indeed seek to show him in just this light. The point to be registered here is not whether such accounts are true or can be verified, but rather whether they capture something of the tenor of the protagonist of Ecclesiastes in a Solomonic form.

5 Weeks, "Solomon and Qoheleth," 74.
6 Weeks, "Solomon and Qoheleth," 71.

The Talmud[7] says that Solomon, having brought the demon Asmodeus to Jerusalem (likely a reference to his worshiping false gods), is hurled a great distance by him (such is the reward of false worship) and has to find his way back as a beggar, his name having been taken away and assumed by the demon. He is called instead Koheleth. The Targum account is similar:

> When King Solomon was sitting upon the throne of his kingdom, his heart became very proud of his riches, and he transgressed the word of God, and he gathered many horses, and chariots, and riders, and he amassed much gold and silver, and he married from foreign nations, whereupon the anger of the Lord was kindled against him, and he sent to him [Asmodeus] the king of the demons, who drove him from the throne of his kingdom, and took away the ring from his hand, in order that he should roam and wander about in the world to reprove it; and he went about in the provincial towns and the cities of the land of Israel, weeping and lamenting, and saying, I am [K]oheleth, whose name was formerly called Solomon, who was king over Israel in Jerusalem.[8]

Versions of this story will get amplified and extended in Jewish and Christian sources. In his commentary on Ecclesiastes 1:12 Jerome says, "The Jews say that this is a book of Solomon's doing penance, because having placed his trust in wisdom and wealth, he gave offense to God by (his) wives."[9] Or Rashi in the Middle Ages, "King Solomon, having experienced both the world's glories and disappointments, wrote the Book of Ecclesiastes in old age to teach the futility of worldly strivings and

[7] b. Gittin 68b.

[8] Tg. Eccl. 1:12, trans. C. D. Ginsburg (1861), available on Sefaria at https://www.sefaria.org/Ecclesiastes.1?lang=bi&p2=Aramaic_Targum_to_Ecclesiastes.1.1&lang2=bi.

[9] Jerome, *Comm. Eccl.* 1:12, in *Proverbs, Ecclesiastes, Song of Solomon*, ed. J. Robert Wright, ACCS 9 (IVP Academic, 2005).

the insignificance of earthly goods."[10] The reception history of Ecclesiastes is heard in conjunction with what is being said in Kings and Chronicles, and potentiality is drawn forth and given literary form. For Weeks, by contrast, the reception history exists to show us departures from the pure isotope, the book of Ecclesiastes, in the form he holds that to be.

In the canonical model of interpretation, the Scriptures, belonging to a community of faith, have undergone supplementation and editing inside the "pure form" already. Weeks does not seek to pare away this editing in the manner of nineteenth-century interpreters but prefers to pare away any subsequent (post–final form) usage as discontinuous with Ecclesiastes and the interpretation proper to it.

For Childs and others working in the domain of reception history, another possibility is at hand. The history of interpretation is a sort of cousin-once-removed to canonical shaping (e.g., the epilogue of Ecclesiastes) at work in the book. So this reception history is worthy of examination for what it wants us to see; that dimension is kept alongside and not viewed in terms of its misreading or comical curiosity.

In his 1974 Exodus commentary Childs broke new ground by including a section on the history of interpretation. At first glance we might ask: What did this have to do with the detailed investment exhibited in the exegetical section itself, and its close examination of source-critical, form-critical, tradition-historical, redaction-critical dimensions of the text, this followed by his newly conceived canonical reflections? The first and largest section belonged firmly on the terrain of modern critical biblical scholarship. To embark on a survey of the earlier history of interpretation would appear to be going backwards, not to mention entering the very terrain

[10] Quoted in Michael V. Fox, *Ecclesiastes: The Traditional Hebrew Text with the New JPS Translation*, JPS Bible Commentary (Jewish Publication Society, 2004), xxv. As Fox notes, this is actually from the medieval Midrash, but it sums up Rashi's view too.

historical criticism was jettisoning so as to do its special "scientific" work.

And I think it fair to say that many who bought the commentary and used it with profit did so out of respect for the hard labor going into the critical evaluation, and less for his "canonical" observations. As for reception history, this showed Childs's impressive command of the history of ideas but was a confusion of the division of labor inhabiting the scholarship of the day, something tacked on but of unclear value.

Childs's own stated reason for surveying the history of interpretation was due to certain similarities he felt it displayed with the depth-dimension of the text, which formed the heart of his labors in the run-up to canonical observations. Just as the scriptural text had a preliminary life in the form of its coming-to-be in the life of a community of inspired tradents and editors, so too it has a rich afterlife in communities of faith reading it "from faith to faith." It belongs to the character of Scripture that it is *never* an artefact but a living word, calling forth response in accordance with its theological and ethical claims. It does that in route to the final form such as we have it, in its life first with the elect family of Israel and now in church and synagogue seeking to hear God's word.[11]

The history of interpretation stands, of course, at a different place in time. "We are not prophets or apostles" but come to the text on the basis of their elected purpose. We are not unfortunate latecomers but rather those who now have a rich

[11] "The section on the history of exegesis offers an analogy to the section on the text's prehistory. The one deals with the period before the text's complete formation, the other with its interpretation after its formation. Both have a significant, albeit indirect, relationship to the major exegetical task of interpreting the canonical text. The history of exegesis is of special interest in illuminating the text by showing how the questions which are brought to bear by subsequent generations of interpreters influenced the answers which they received. No one comes to the text de novo, but consciously or unconsciously shares a tradition with his predecessors. This section therefore tries to bring some historical controls to the issue of how the present generation is influenced by the exegetical traditions in which we now stand" (Brevard S. Childs, *Exodus*, OTL [Westminster, 1974], xv).

two-testament witness that, in point of historical fact, the first hearers did not have. The Jewish community has its own scriptural foundation and the subsequent testimony of written sages. We do not read this rich heritage and substitute it for the canonical form of Scripture, but seek to understand how we too belong to a community of faith that lives alongside it and joins in the credal affirmation, "We believe in one, holy, catholic and apostolic church."[12]

Just as with the diachronic preliminary life of Scripture, its role is in sharpening our eye on the canonical form. The history of interpretation, as well, places before us what faithful readers alongside us in the church have heard, asking that the inspiration of Scripture guide and inform our interpretation. On this account, the traditions associating Solomon and Ecclesiastes, or the hearing of Ecclesiastes in specific liturgical settings, are the outworking of Scripture as it reaches into a living context guided by its authority. We are not drawing hard historical conclusions about whether the stories of Solomon can find evidentiary confirmation; that is not what they are about as a genre. The traditions seek to "hear" Ecclesiastes in relationship to the narratives of Kings and in the canonical context of all three works associated with him. We spoke of the latter context in the chapter preceding. And this "hearing" is on a different but related plane to how the book of Ecclesiastes itself comes to form. Ecclesiastes is a book "authored" by Solomon in only the most oblique sense of the term.

We can see this insight confirmed as well in the history of interpretation, when we exit the preoccupations of modern historical reading and look at an age not our own. The rationalist hermeneutic of a legal mind like that of Grotius gave rise to enormous counterforces, seeking to secure Ecclesiastes as the

[12] Brevard S. Childs, *The Struggle to Understand Isaiah as Christian Scripture* (Eerdmans, 2014), 323: "By reviewing the history of the church's biblical interpretation, we can derive new confidence in confessing with the church, I believe in the one holy catholic and apostolic church." I have a fuller discussion in *Convergences: Canon and Catholicity* (Baylor University Press, 2020), 93–122.

actual work of King Solomon. When one looks at a different era it becomes clear that what was regarded in early modernity as a pious defense of Solomon gave as well as took away.

One of the earliest commentaries we have, that of Didymus the Blind, will pose the question directly. "Are the words of Ecclesiastes said by the author personally?" He answers in this way and then moves briskly on:

> Actually, the Spirit is the author of the divinely inspired Scriptures . . . Either the real author is Solomon, or some other wise man may have written it. Maybe we should opt for the latter so that nobody may say the speaker talks about himself.[13]

The comment is compressed. He is asking who is inspired by God to set this work before us. He thinks the attribution to Solomon would overdetermine how we read the book. The inspiration of Ecclesiastes would be limited if it were Solomon simply talking about himself, as Didymus sees it. Divine inspiration belongs to a higher plane of communication, we can infer. It is more than simply speaking about oneself.

The Counsels of Wisdom and Fouquet

There are three works that circulate around the period of Fouquet's imprisonment that are anonymous compositions. *Le Théologien dans les conversations avec les sages et les grands du monde* (1683); *Les Conseils de la Sagesse* (1677 and an expanded version in 1683); *Méthode pour converser avec Dieu* (1687). We might well conclude that the success of a work is not as reliant on the author writing it as it is on the subject matter itself. Two of these works will find later attribution to Michel Boutauld and Pierre Coton, both Jesuits. Even here there is confusion, as in this notice:

> Boutauld, Michel, a French Jesuit preacher, was born in Paris, Nov. 2, 1625. He died at Pontoise, May 16, 1688,

[13] Didymus the Blind, *Commentary on Ecclesiastes*, in *Proverbs, Ecclesiastes, Song of Solomon*, ed. J. Robert Wright, ACCS 9 (IVP Academic, 2005), 192.

> leaving some works which are much esteemed: *Les Conseils de la Sagesse* (Paris, 1677, 12mo):—*Suite de Ditto* (ibid. 1683, 12mo; the last edition is of 1749): *Le Theologien des Conversations avec les Sages*, etc. (1683).[14]

Le Théologien is now customarily attributed to the earlier and better-known Pierre Coton S.J. (1564–1626), as it locates its discourses in the reign of Henry IV.

Well into the nineteenth century, French historians will continue to defend the authorship of the *Counsels* as written by Nicolas Fouquet. We have examined a major early English edition where the link to Fouquet is central to how we are to read the book. Apparently, the person responsible for the attribution to Boutauld is one Père Sommervogel, a Jesuit, in a work published under another name(!).

> Ce livre a été longtemps attribué au célèbre surintendant Nicolas Fouquet, et cela jusqu'en 1862, par Chéruel, dans ses "Mémoires sur la vie publique et privée de Fouquet." Sommervogel qui défend sa tribu, a tranché dans son article N. Fouquet théologien (sous le pseudonyme de P. Clauer) paru dans *l'Ami des livres de René Muffat* (1862). Il attribue définitivement le livre au jésuite Boutauld (1604–1689).

> For a long time, this book was attributed to the celebrated Nicolas Fouquet, indeed up to 1862 by Chéruel in his "Mémoires sur la vie publique et privée de Fouquet." Sommervogel who takes the position of his tribe (the Jesuits), thus declared in his essay "N. Fouquet the theologian" (under the pseudonym of one P. Clauer) in *l'Ami des livres de René Muffat* (1862). He attributed the work definitively to the Jesuit Boutauld (1604–1689).[15]

[14] This is the entry given in a typical internet search (there is very little to be found, for reasons explored in appendix 1 below).

[15] Urbain-Victor Chatelain, *Le Surintendant Nicolas Foucquet, protecteur des lettres des arts et des sciences* (Perrin, 1905), 546–47.

This attribution is rejected by Chatelain and seen as reasonable by Petitfils. It is a debate without a lot of clues. (Petitfils, writing a century later, has access to the timeline on which we can plot Fouquet's access to paper and writing.) How Sommervogel is able to make this attribution two centuries after the publication of the *Counsels* is intriguing in and of itself. Who is the seventeenth-century Jesuit? Reading the one work attributed to him without any controversy (*Méthode*, 1689), it would be hard on that basis alone to deduce that he wrote *Counsels*. It is a charming book and full of spiritual insight, but nothing in its contents would help identify him as the author of the anonymous 1677 volume.[16]

What we do know is that the 1677 preface wants us to read the book as composed in a solitary exile. First readers did that and concluded that Fouquet was the author. Generations of readers did the same, and with confidence and commendation. In the essay to which we have been referring, Weeks writes this:

> The *Conseils de la Sagesse*, incidentally, is interesting in another respect. It is now generally attributed to the little-known Michel Boutauld, but it was published anonymously, and in his preface the author portrays himself as a man exiled to a lonely place . . . The more interesting point is that this book seems almost universally to have been attributed by early readers to Nicolas Fouquet, the fabulously wealthy and extravagant Superintendent of Finances in France under Louis XIV, who suffered a sudden and spectacular fall from grace, eventually finding himself imprisoned in the fortress of Pignerol, and cut off from his previous life.

This is of course consistent with the position of the present book and the question we are pursuing concerning authorship

[16] I lay out the basic issues in appendix 1 below. The work by Michel Boutauld, *Méthode pour converser avec Dieu*, réédition au XIXème siècle ([1689] Ch. Amat, 1899), is widely available in reprint form.

and attribution as hermeneutical indexes. He then adds this line:

> This identification, which may have contributed to the popularity of the book, clearly rests not solely on the author's own vague mentions of his solitude, but on an association with Solomon's fall, to which he makes no reference himself.[17]

This of course elides the entire force of the preface to the *Counsels*, which means to tell us how to read the contents to follow: as the reflections of a man who has faced exile and adversity but has found God inside of and because of that. Any reader would read his story in light of the Solomon who speaks in the "counsels of wisdom" that constitute the book in their hands.

It is to Weeks's credit that he is aware of the significance of the work and its subsequent reception history.

> This work, and a sequel that came to be presented as its second volume, multiple editions in French throughout the following century, and it was translated into English and German four times each, Latin at least three times, Dutch and Spanish twice, Swedish, Italian, Polish, Greek, Portuguese, and Russian. By any standards this was a very successful book . . .[18]

It is not clear to me what the final line quoted above intends to say in respect of the book's popularity. As we saw above in the extensive commendation by the English translator J. Leake, the book does indeed gain its popularity on the basis of the preface with its mention of the exile of Fouquet. Leake does not say anything about Solomon's fall, however, in his remarks. And *Counsels* draws no particular attention to it. To the degree that the general public might make that inference,

[17] Weeks, "Solomon and Qoheleth," 276.

[18] Weeks, "Solomon and Qoheleth," 276; see also the exhaustive bibliography prepared by Weeks in *The Making of Many Books: Printed Works on Ecclesiastes 1523–1875* (Eisenbrauns, 2014), 69–70.

it would simply be on the basis of a general sensibility already formed in their minds.

A more economical account of the matter is that the story of the fall of Fouquet was what was well known. This is consistent with Leake's writing in the decades following his death. Fouquet's career, his rise and fall, had its own compelling character. What *Counsels* brings to the picture is, as the subtitle puts it, "a collection of the sayings from Solomon which are most necessary for a man to conduct himself wisely, with reflections on those sayings." The fall, the imprisonment, the adversity faced—these events were all well known. What is given amplification is the wisdom gained by a man in such a situation. What Leake infers on the basis of *Counsels* and public knowledge is that Fouquet learned penitence and humility through adversity. His "fall" was not the last word. By no means. We have looked at his account in detail above.

Because we are now able to see far more of Fouquet's last years than could have been inferred by the author of the preface or the author of the English language commendation (1734), we find surprising independent confirmation of what they could only surmise. Fouquet is indeed a man of contrition and spiritual wisdom gained through extreme adversity, an isolation of nearly two decades, separation from his loved ones, his previous career traumatically brought to a close, now left alone with God, devotional writings, Scripture, and a conscience seeking forgiveness and peace.

We do not know what happened to Solomon after the last chapter of the account of the Deuteronomistic Historian. That record ends with him bringing ruin about his head, worshiping false gods and allowing his previous devotion to God to be replaced by foolish alliances with foreign wives. In our view, the author Ecclesiastes has sought to give Solomon voice beyond the close of the historical record. The content of what he says is closer to the known writings of Fouquet than the material attributed to him in *The Counsels of Wisdom*, even as it is a particular and distinctive Solomonic confession. The technique, the giving voice to well-known figures in the public memory at the end of their lives, is the same.

As stated in the introductory chapter, *Counsels* becomes a testimony to Fouquet in the same way that Ecclesiastes evokes and bears witness to a Solomon at the end of his days. Fouquet has lost his previously vain life and found a spiritually elevated life borne witness to in the wisdom of the Scriptures and time alone with God.

Why did Michel Boutauld S.J., presuming he is the author, seek to have this work, consisting of Solomon's sayings and meditations on them, be presented as Fouquet's exilic reflections on wisdom, kingship, and God? We have noted the interest those in Paris continued to have in the exiled former superintendent. Historians can fill out this picture and note the affairs at court, and the intrigues constantly whirling around, that might explain why in time Louis XIV becomes more lenient toward this man he condemned to life imprisonment.

We can also recall the faithfulness of a mother and a wife, to which Fouquet makes reference, and their known lives of prayer and devotion. Fouquet mentions this at the very start of his last letter to his wife: "Nothing moves me so much as the cares you have taken over our chapel and the devotions you make there."[19] Perhaps the unknown Boutauld was a friend of Madame Fouquet, the founder of the chapel to which his body was brought a year after his death. Did he know Fouquet during his years of education at the Collège de Clermont, the Jesuit school in Paris where a young man learned enough Latin to translate the Psalms many years later in Pignerol?

We do not know who Boutauld was any more than we know who composed Ecclesiastes. He intended *Counsels* to be seen as reflections coming from the exiled Fouquet in what would be three years before his death. The author of Ecclesiastes has sought something of the same for Koheleth, the

[19] Charles Drazin, *The Man Who Outshone the Sun King: Ambition, Triumph and Treachery in the Reign of Louis XIV* (Random House, 2009), 292.

erstwhile king and accumulator who had lost his name, as later stories of Solomon would have it.

Early in his days at Pignerol, his former servant and a friend from Provence sought to meet the imprisoned Fouquet. He threw some messages from the window. In a twist of fate, he might just as well have thrown from his window a volume of enormous popularity that would become associated with his name, and would remain so for centuries.

The man without a name—the Man in the Iron Mask—would ironically fill the annals of speculation and recreation beyond his wildest dreams. The man with a name, as great as the Sun King himself, would lose his name. But as with anyone truly Predestinate, that would not be the last word. More was required to be said. *The Counsels of Wisdom* speaks for Fouquet, no matter who wrote it, just as Ecclesiastes speaks for the king who lost his name.

8
Koheleth and Fouquet
The End of the Matter

My wife Elizabeth and I lived for four years in the rectory of a twelfth-century Catholic parish church in the tiny village of Courances. Today the village is best known for its chateau built in 1630 in pure Louis XIII style. The attribution of the very special grounds to André Le Nôtre, famous landscape architect of Vaux-le-Vicomte, including the long canal and water features, is "undocumented and dubious." The grounds are lavish and beautiful all the same, and the horseshoe entry staircase will put you in mind of the one at the Cour des Adieux in Fontainebleau, where Napoleon said his final goodbyes. Courances and Vaux share being lesser known than Versailles. Both are more charming and more genuinely French. One can imagine real life there, and not the Sun King pacing the grounds laid out by Le Nôtre as if God himself.

My wife was running a French culture, language, and travel business and so the opportunities to visit Vaux-le-Vicomte were frequent and always a pleasure. It is but a half-hour away. I have inherited and continued her splendid work.

I am often asked about day trips for clients in Paris, and invariably I recommend Vaux. The guide we work with is very good. My late mother and youngest brother came for a visit at the time my wife was recovering from a lung transplant in Paris, and it was an easy call to opt to visit Fouquet's grand achievement. I always love seeing the French schoolchildren visiting. The site attendants provide period costumes for them, and nothing is more pleasurable than seeing them strut their finery. One can imagine them as child stand-ins for the guests attending the fateful dinner on the night of August 17, 1659.

I started this journey with Fouquet and Ecclesiastes by recounting a visit to the Marais, to the chapel that is his final resting place. Services were underway in what is now a Protestant *temple*, and because the church representatives, while wanting to be helpful, knew nothing of Fouquet or the history of their worship edifice, I was left puzzled as to why he is unknown in the very church associated with his mother and family. The passing of the years is of course one explanation, and the curious disposition of the chapel of the Sisters of the Visitation falling into the hands of a very different church ownership after the Revolution. The average educated French person will know Fouquet's name and something of his history. They are not likely, however, to know where he is buried. Pignerol imprisonment was something of the last stop of Nicolas Fouquet.

In doing some further research, my instinct that I was not in the company of those best placed to know the history of the building where they gathered to worship has proven correct. I was not in doubt that his body was resting there—all standard sources say as much. I was less sure, especially after speaking with them, that there was something like general access to his tomb and what one might assume were the plaques and notices stipulating this. I had read the final death notices and wanted to see if they were on view. The foreign-language worship service underway preoccupied them, and I was unable to determine the physical disposition of the place, even as I tried to inquire about it.

Upon return to my home in the United States, I phoned the Sisters of the Visitation, now located on the Left Bank near the Luxembourg Gardens. A quiet voice responded on the other end of the line to me and my questions about Fouquet and his inhumation. No, they could not help me.

In the fine biography of Petitfils, he records the following:

> On 9 April 1680, Louvais authorized the Governor (Saint-Mars) to remit the body to his family with permission to have it transported "where it seemed good to them." The body was initially placed at the Convent of Saint-Claire in Pignerol. In March of 1681, it was conveyed to Paris for a commemorative Mass at the end of the year . . . and put down into the family crypt of the Convent of the Ladies of Holy Mary, rue Saint-Antoine. We do not know if Marie de Maupeou (his mother) attended the ceremony. She died one month later on 22 April 1681, at age 81, in "les dehors du Val-de Grâce" where she had retired.[1]

He continues:

> In the archives of the Visitation one can find a text making reference to this ceremony, owing to the pen of a religious charged with chronicling affairs for the monastery: Nicolas Fouquet, as is recorded, died at Pignerol in the month of March 1680, at the age of sixty-five. His family had his body brought back here at great cost: he was deposited in our church, which was draped in black from the vault to the floor. He was *inhumé* in the same grotto where Monsieur his father had been placed forty years earlier. The grotto of the Fouquet family is still located in the crypt of the church, to the left of the entrance, under the Chapel of St. Francis de Sales.

Here Petitfils speaks of efforts to make sure that the body is genuinely his and confirm the facts of his death, given rumors otherwise that he has reviewed and rejected.

He continues:

[1] Jean-Christian Petitfils, *Fouquet* (Perrin, 1998), 511.

> One will find the sepulchers of seven members of the family. Francois IV, father of Nicolas; Yves and Basile, his sons; François and Louis Nicolas, his grandchildren, sons of Nicolas; Louise Fourché et Marie-Madeleine de Castille, first and second wives of Nicolas. The eighth casket, anonymous, was that of Superintendent Fouquet: as with all prisoners of the State dying in captivity, this latter forfeited his identity. In the eyes of the King and of the world, he was dead civilly on the day of his condemnation at trial.[2]

Hence the sad reality that, though I was able to locate the chapel building, and its "historical monument plaque" on the façade stating the religious origins of the building, nothing was to the public eye stated about the most renowned man now resting there. Louis XIV took him away in 1662 and sought to erase his name by that act.

The final words spoken over Fouquet the man come from the death notice prepared by the Sisters of the Visitation. I quoted a portion of them in the introductory chapter. Here they are in full, with some commentary by the biographer Petitfils.

> On 28 March 1681, Monsieur Nicolas Foucquet was buried in our church, in the chapel of Saint Francis de Sales, a man elevated to every degree of honor in government, attorney-general of the Parlement, Master of Requests, Procurer General, Superintendent of Finances, and Minister of State. In the great offices he held, he demonstrated so extraordinary a talent, so noble a manner and such just and generous feeling, that the past centuries can offer almost no one to rival his accomplishments. But God, who wanted to make a Predestinate, overturned all these great earthly achievements. He was disgraced, in spite of his important services, put on trial

[2] Petitfils, *Fouquet*, 512–13.

> and imprisoned for more than eighteen years. It was during these trials that, stripped of all his honors, he rediscovered virtue and experienced the enlightenment of faith. He began to open his eyes and to recognize the emptiness of worldly splendors. He renounced these vanities so that eternal truth and the most pure light of the Gospel might fill his mind and his heart. His most important occupations were given over to reading, prayer and frequenting the holy sacraments. Finally, from a man obsessed with everything that is great and vain in the world, he becomes, by the spirit of God, perfectly instructed and touched by what is most holy in religion. So it was that by his disgrace he changed his ways, achieved sanctity and died, full of good deeds and righteousness before God.[3]

Jean-Christian Petitfils, a sober historian, is wrapping up this final chapter on the last things pertaining to the life and death of Nicolas Fouquet. One senses that he has been caught up in the grand itinerary of this man's life, its heights and depths, and the final years illuminating an altogether different frame of mind.

He concludes in this way:

> Despite some excesses in expression, the text of this obituary has the great merit of highlighting an aspect of Nicolas Fouquet's life that the historian cannot forget: that his ardent, passionate, brilliant and extraordinary existence, which knew prosperity and misfortune, greatness and disgrace, was also a spiritual journey worthy of "the great century of saints" which had seen it born: a patient and serene search for humility after vain years of pride, a fervent quest for divine mercy, accompanied by contrition for the errors of a carefree youth, in short a slow rise from darkness towards the unalterable light of God.[4]

[3] Petitfils, *Fouquet*, 514.
[4] Petitfils, *Fouquet*, 514.

For readers following his career in this small book, the tribute is most fitting. In the language of Ecclesiastes, "The end of the matter, all has been heard." Solomon and Fouquet live on in the works attributed to them.

Conclusion

In the final years of teaching PhD seminars I turned with some seriousness to the book of Ecclesiastes. As it would transpire, three of my final doctoral students all chose to research topics related to the book. You never know anything well until you are asked to teach it, to work your way carefully through the Hebrew text, to find readings that complement and stretch students, and to deal with questions you have not asked yourself but which arise from curious and intelligent minds.

I found that, when it came to the final chapter of the book—as we read it aloud in Hebrew and "sought to find pleasing words" in English to faithfully render the text—the verses of chapter 12 seemed to grab a hold of me spiritually and emotionally. It was as if it were accomplishing the act of dying in some very effective way in "the way the words go," the text's *akolouthia* as early hermeneutics termed it. My wife had just got very close to death prior to a necessary lung transplant, and indeed needed to prepare for that before entering the life-or-death realm of a twelve-hour surgery that would hopefully save her life: something that would not be clear until six days of reanimation under careful medical supervision. I shared that experience in my own way as her husband.

Perhaps this accounted for it. We are listening to a narrator describe the death of "the single brooding consciousness" whose journey we have been following: his slowly becoming a different man. From the acknowledgment of the vanity of human accumulation and achievement; to the coming to terms with the eccentricities of the world around him, that his wealth and preoccupations had kept him from looking at, with eyes unaccustomed to their reality; to the coming face to face with mysteries in life for which the only thing to be said is "Who knows?"

To the degree I had been educated to think of the book as a tribute to pessimism and futility, with a man discontented with God and the created world he was inhabiting, the book became monotone and lacking any real life. Death was then a kind of relief, in the same way the commendations of joy would be transformed into "Seize the day, tomorrow we die" cynicisms.

Because my later years of work in Scripture had begun to turn in the direction of the earlier history of interpretation, I had to come to terms with the fact that the book of Ecclesiastes was never heard in this way. The obvious deduction was that it was our own age that was letting this particular way of hearing the book rise up. The readings assigned for the graduate courses I was teaching would begin to include so-called premodern interpretation. Perhaps we needed to go to school and see what other generations had to say about this admittedly "advanced reading" course book.

I stumbled onto *Les Conseils de la Sagesse* and, among other things, was astonished at how this volume had saturated an era. The translational afterlife of the 1677 French edition has been noted above. It was, to use our lingo, a "bestseller." At the time I assumed this had to do with its educational value, for raising children and the like. "How to conduct yourself in life." But this supposition was just a guess, and it was wrong. As we have seen, the book consists of a grand selection of the sayings of Solomon, followed by a paraphrase and a long meditation or reflection.

In the English translation we examined above, the link to Fouquet was certainly instrumental in bringing the book to life. It put flesh and blood on the scriptural deposit and the reflections that followed.

It was because I was living in France at the time, and indeed not far from Vaux-le-Vicomte, that the picture gradually became clearer. I knew the outlines of Fouquet's life, but in nothing like the detail shared here. Fouquet is remembered for the chateau he built and the brilliant team he assembled that made it what it was and is. Because his imprisonment was so long—a full eighteen years—and his fall so precipitous, he vanishes into a kind of lost space and time. There is the glorious chateau and grounds, a lasting tribute. But where is this man, where did he go, and why was his memory so thoroughly made to vanish? We have looked at some poignant reminders of just how cruelly and effectively he lost his name to the larger world.

I realized, or came to be made aware, of the unique intersection of Ecclesiastes and Fouquet the longer I sought to know more about the man in the mask of Pignerol captivity and exile. That *Conseils* bequeathed to history a man unmasked and set free in time again is a fate that probably its mysterious author, whoever people thought he was at the time, could never have imagined it would give to him. In its own way this got me to thinking about things like authorship, inspiration, reception, and how mysteriously they can be brought into a place of purpose much larger than human intention could ever account for.

Who wrote Ecclesiastes? Didymus the Blind brought his internal eyes before that question and thought about it from a different angle. If it were a book about Solomon principally, it would be deprived of its right to be a book much larger than a set of narrow historical markers focused on a king who lived and died. The book wants to see more and say more, and it does this in the freedom of an inspiration seeking to give a man voice as he comes to terms with a life limited by the compass of accumulation and accomplishment swirling around him.

The book only needs to bring our Solomon on stage briefly to accomplish that, and so it does that and then goes its own way.

"Is this the real Solomon speaking?" is a question that makes it sound like "the real Solomon" can in fact be grasped and understood by finding out "who he really was." But Scripture, when it comes to figures like Solomon, is far more interested in who God thinks they are and what role and destiny he allows to unfold at his hand. Ecclesiastes is telling us finally who God thinks Solomon is, and Koheleth is brought onto the stage to let arise a penetrating look at matters inhabiting the soul of rich kings and all those who find themselves so situated in this life "under the sun."

Nicolas Fouquet thought he knew who he was. He was sure with an adamantine certainty that, above all else, he was the loyal, true, devoted servant of the king, who had kept France in financial solvency through extremely hard trials and with truly impressive success. He was not wrong about that. That Louis XIV did not share that view does not make him right and Fouquet wrong. It just means he was the king and Fouquet was his subject. The king can put his thumb on the scales of a relatively fair trial and send him away for life in a remote fortress below the Italian Alps, because that is his royal prerogative. And so he did.

His decisions to act more leniently toward Fouquet are not the function of God getting through to him and altering his bearing and disposition. A man walking the vast gardens of Versailles as though it is a sundial and he is the sun is for all intents and purposes lost to God.

Fouquet is not walking on a garden sundial, but he is walking on a path that God has laid out for those who seek after him and find him, through steady devotion, through adversity, through the reckonings of a conscience and a memory guided by the merciful Judge of all the world and of all time. He did not know who he was, just to the degree he was the "inspired author" of his own life. God had a story he wanted Fouquet to read, and lo and behold it was the story God was writing about him.

As the Sisters of the Visitation put it, "But God, who wanted to make a Predestinate, overturned all these great earthly achievements." Fouquet found out who he was. Ecclesiastes "found out" who Solomon was. About both of them we see God writing a story they could never have written about themselves. For each man in his own unique way, to a purpose unique to each: God wanted to make a Predestinate.

Appendix 1
Authorship in the Seventeenth Century

The following notes, which I have translated into English, came to me by private correspondence from Patrick Goujon S.J., Professor of Theology and the History of Spirituality at Facultés Loyola Paris. He is responding to questions I posed about (1) anonymous publications in the seventeenth century, (2) the concept of an author in this period, (3) how a nineteenth-century Jesuit attributed *Conseils* to a contemporary of Fouquet's, one Michel Boutauld, and (4) who this man might be and more importantly why he would construct a preface intimating the authorship of Fouquet.

On this latter point, his speculations line up with the position I take in my book. My translations of his communication with me follow.

He writes:

1. "The notion of 'the author' fluctuated greatly in the seventeenth century. Due to the development and distribution of printed works during this century, its character began to be defined. Still, the notion was at most nascent, though the legal and commercial realities would slowly bring about a change. We can see this in works from the Middle Ages whose attributions were uncertain in the nature of the case. In the seventeenth century this could begin to change. Printed works also began to receive prefaces which intimated authorship. A preface might attribute a text to an

author for any reason. If the maxims of Solomon received an attributing preface, this is fascinating from the standpoint of literary and more general historiography. On the one hand, Fouquet becomes a sort of legitimized figure of the nobility, opposed to royalty, a theme we have often forgotten due to the ensuing French Revolution, which sees the driving force as 'the people.' The protesting nobility played as much, if not more, of a role. Publishing a work of Christian morality, and wisdom, under the name of Fouquet (or insinuated by means of a preface), could participate both in this legitimization and also allow for a 'commercial coup': Here is a book by the great Fouquet."

2. "The relationship between Fouquet and the Jesuits deserves to be explored, but here, I am fairly certain that nothing has been written. Fouquet was a student of the Jesuits at the Collège de Clermont in Paris, and he is a few years from the same generation as Boutauld. Did they know each other, was the Jesuit the 'tutor' of young Fouquet? We are at the limit of what can be known."

3. "In fact, it is very unlikely that a noble, of this high rank, would have had [in the course of a normal life] the idea of writing and publishing. This would have been viewed as a fall from the title of nobility. Only memoirs could be imagined, but here again the few more-or-less contemporary equivalents show that this was not self-evident."

4. "Sommervogel, a Jesuit scholar of the nineteenth century, in fact wrote the entire catalog of the works of the Jesuits, which was initially intended only as a list of corrections and clarifications of a directory of works then published by a major Parisian publisher, in no way religious. With very rare exceptions, these judgments are always considered valid. He is part of this generation of European intellectuals linked to the encyclopedism of the nineteenth century, these great repertoires established in all fields. The 'Sommervogel' is known by historians as a reliable work, undoubtedly not immune to errors and omissions of course" (see below).

5. "The *Bibliothèque nationale de France* (BNF) notice for *Conseils* indicates that the first editions came from the publisher Mabre-Cramoisy. The latter was the main publication house of the Jesuits, a printer also closely linked to the Parisian royal and parliamentary power, which again would argue against the publication of a book by Fouquet. (As I understand it, the first edition, in 1677, of the *Conseils* was without the author's name, but a handwritten note will later attribute it to the Jesuit Boutauld. After the success of another book by Boutauld, *Méthode pour converser avec Dieu*, 1678, it is under this same name that the main editions of the *Conseils* were published in the nineteenth century.)"
6. "In conclusion, but as a hypothesis of course, I therefore think that the work of *Conseils* is indeed by Boutauld, and that it is a later attribution, via this preface, which makes Fouquet to be the 'author.'"

In roaming the internet I also came across this note, which links Louvois to the Collège of Clermont. We note in the discussion above the close friendship which will evolve between Fouquet and Louvois. The latter is twenty-seven years younger than Fouquet. They have similar career paths, and this may have contributed to what over the course of time became a warm relationship. Fouquet successfully helped him with a medical condition of the eyes.

> The letter to Saint-Mars, which was dated 19 July 1669, was written on the orders of Louis XIV by François-Michel Le Tellier, marquis de Louvois. Still only twenty-eight years old, Louvois was destined to play a vital role in the story of the Man in the Iron Mask. Serving as Louis XIV's minister of state for war, Louvois had been educated at the Jesuit Collège de Clermont in the rue Saint-Jacques in Paris. Upon leaving the school in 1657, he was instructed in French law by his father, the formidable secretary of state for war, Michel Le Tellier. Louvois then served at the parlement of Metz as counsellor before

> obtaining the survivance of his father's office. He worked in the ministry for war for a time, learning the job under his father's guidance, but Le Tellier would hand over increasing amounts of ministry work to his son and, upon being made chancellor in 1677, he would leave Louvois in sole charge. As the minister for war, the garrison and prison of Pignerol came under Louvois's jurisdiction, as did any prisoner who might be held there.[1]

On Fouquet as the seventeenth-century author of *Les Conseils* see Carlos Sommervogel, *Bibliothéque de la Compagnie de Jesus*, nouvelle ed. (Picard, 1841), 47:

> *Les Conseils de la Sagesse* ont été attribués au celèbre Fouquet, mais cette opinion doit être abandonée. Elle a été soutenue de nouveau en 1802 par M. Chéruel dans ses Memoires sur la vie publique et privée de Fouquet, et cela malgré la décision de Barbier. Bien plus, M. Chéruel dépouille le P. Boutauld de ses deux autres ouvrages, pour les donner encore à Fouquet. Cette question me semble avoir été tranchée dans un article: *Nicolas Fouquet théologien* . . . (Paris, 1862).

> *The Counsels of Wisdom* have been attributed to the famous Fouquet, but this opinion must be abandoned. It was supported again in 1802 by Monsieur Chéruel in his *Memoirs on the public and private life of Fouquet*, despite Barbier's decision. Moreover, Monsieur Chéruel strips Father Boutauld of his two other works, to give them again to Fouquet. This question seems to me to have been resolved in an article: *Nicolas Fouquet theologue* . . . (Paris, 1862).

Incidentally, I translate the discussion from Chatelain (1902) on this controverted topic in chapter 2 above. Chatelain agrees

[1] Josephine Wilkinson, *The Man in the Iron Mask: The Truth About Europe's Most Famous Prisoner* (Pegasus Books, 2021).

with Chéruel on the attribution to Fouquet, but says about "the two other works" that one was correctly assigned by Sommervogel, not to Boutauld, but to one Père Coton. See the note above.

Professor Goujon on question 3:

7. Sommervogel compiled bibliographies that already existed (from the eighteenth century, "la bibliothèque de . . .") and the Jesuit order has had, since the beginning, the custom of taking record of everything. Each Jesuit needed to ask permission to publish from his provincial, and the latter had an annual record of each book published, a copy of which was transferred to Rome. Since the sixteenth century, this helped the Jesuits publish their own "bibliography." We have the largest religious archives in the world (not being the oldest one, but the more centralized one). Fortunately (not for historians) a lot of things also disappeared.

There is an excellent doctoral dissertation by Robert Danieluk S.J., who is himself an archivist of the General Curia in Rome.[2]

I subsequently purchased a reprint volume of Boutauld's *Méthode pour converser avec Dieu.* It comes from the thirteenth edition made in 1770, that is, roughly a century after Fouquet's death. The printer has provided this interesting note in the form of a preface. He says that a reader will not fail to spot places that appear word for word in two other works, including *Counsels.* Intriguingly, it will later be determined that the other volume (*Le Théologien*) was not the work of Boutauld (see the discussion above concerning the views of Chatelain). One can see how untangling these matters would take some time and entail considerable confusion.

[2] "L'écriture de l'histoire de la Compagnie de Jésus: L'œuvre bibliographique de Carlos Sommervogel (1890–1932)," description available in the *Annuaires de l'École pratique des hautes études* 113 (2004): 389–91, https://www.persee.fr/doc/ephe_0000-0002_2004_num_117_113_12390.

From *Méthode pour converser avec Dieu* (13th ed., 1770).

Avertissement de l'imprimeur. Cette *Méthode* est de l'auteur de deux livres assez connus dans le monde: *Les Conseils de la Sagesse* et *le Théologien dans les Conversations*: c'est pourquoi le Lecteur ne fera pas surpris s'il trouve dans celui-ci quelques endroits ou un peu imités, ou même tirés mot à mot des deux autres. La vue de l'Auteur a été en cela, de remmetre devant les yeux des personnes devotés, et dans un volume encore plus commode que des *Conseils de la Sagesse*, les pensées les plus touchantes qui sont répandues dans cet Ouvrage sur la matiere qu'il traite ici; et on ne doit pas douter qu'il n'y ait réussi parfaitement après les bénédictions qu'il a plu à Dieu de donner à tout ce qui est forti de sa plume.

Printer's warning. This *Method* (*of Conversing with God*) is from the author of two books quite well known in the world: *The Counsels of Wisdom* and *The Theologian in Conversations*: this is why the Reader will not be surprised if he finds in this book some places where a little is imitated, or even taken word for word from the other two. The intention of the Author was in this way, to place before the eyes of devout people, and in a volume even more convenient than the *Counsels of Wisdom*, the most apposite thoughts which are set forth in this work on the matter that he deals with here; and we must not doubt that he succeeded perfectly after the blessings which it pleased God to give to all who were strengthened by his pen.

Appendix 2

Arrival at Pignerol Prison: Snapshot of the First Ten Years

From Paul Morand, *Fouquet, ou le soleil offusqué*, chapter 16, "The Dungeon of Pignerol" (pp. 153–60) and his concluding remarks (pp. 176–78). Excerpts.

> In the open Piedmont, the village of Pignerol rose up in the clouds, between denuded mountains, chilled to the bone by rain and snow. In deepest winter, a black interior of a white prison. D'Artagnan did not want to remain there. "I prefer a simple soldier to being a jailor," he had told Colbert, who replied, "Go tell that to the King if you dare." D'Artagnan did dare and the King did not take offense. "I have more regard," he said, "for the office of jailor than that of a soldier." Saint-Mars, d'Artagnan's lieutenant, placed Fouquet among the prisoners.
>
> After four thousand acres at Vaux, two rooms six feet long, this was a change. Forbidden to walk, no visits, no ink, no paper. One confessor, but from the region. Pecquet, his private physician, had offered to go and share the confinement with Fouquet; he was refused; news from his family authorized but two times per year.
>
> At Paris, the Court of Justice was dissolved, the creditors unionized. France had a Master. That was all Pignerol knew of the outside world. But as for Fouquet himself, he did not know even that.

> *The Counsels of Wisdom* were attributed to Fouquet, to have been composed by him in prison. He translated Psalm 118. "Fouquet is as a lamb," said Saint-Mars. The prisoner prayed. The return to the faith of youth is the natural bent of misfortune. Distanced from his wife and his mother, of their faith so firm, he was subject to their distant influence; the dead and the absent become the beings most loved. He tried to imitate Monsieur Vincent, who died a saintly death, saying only one word, *confido*, "I trust." He recalled the teachings of the Jesuits who raised him: "Make around you the desert," a maxim that they were the first to apply to the Jansenists.
>
> Toward the end of ten years in exclusion (October 1672), Louvois authorized Saint-Mars to remit to Fouquet two memoranda from his wife (having to do with financial affairs).

Morand concludes this chapter thus:

> Mme Fouquet intervened again with Louis XIV, that she be allowed to go to Pignerol to share her husband's captivity: the king refused. Fouquet, however, succeeded in sending his wife a letter which circulated in Paris, among his friends.
>
> Thinking of death, which he feels is not far away, he implores her to continue to do everything possible for his enlargement, speaks of his children, of his valets who died in Pignerol, "the air of the citadel being always in some excess . . ." "There is no evil in a human body from which I do not feel some attack . . ." He looks as if four days dead. Sciatica, colic, gravel, ruined teeth, no longer able to see without glasses . . . "How you would find him different from himself," says the Elegy.

Final chapter, concerning Fouquet's death, eight years later:

> The king had just accorded to Fouquet his freedom, and permission to go take the waters at Bourbon, when

> he fell as struck by lightning into the arms of his son, "after convulsions, heart strain, unable to vomit" (so Mme Sévigné), he died on 23 March 1680, at the age of sixty-five.

He concludes:

> Fouquet dead, from whom his last daughter was stolen, Colbert alive, surrounded by his daughters, all three duchesses, this recasting of destinies seems too perfect, accomplished to the point of strangeness; it is nevertheless logical, moral, luminous: the impatient man was blocked, the man who waited for his hour found it; the goods of this world slipped from the hands of the first into those of the second.
>
> But Fouquet saved his life, leaving Colbert condemned to row in the galley ship of the vain world, with perfumed gloves.
>
> The gods do not like a happy man.

From the cover of his book we read:

> Fouquet must have believed that everything can be bought, even destiny. Fouquet is the liveliest, most natural, most tolerant, most brilliant man, the most gifted in the art of living, the most French. He will be caught in a vice, between two proud, dry, cautious, secretive, merciless purifiers, Louis XIV and Colbert. He will succumb, having remained a man from the time of the Fronde, living in a disordered France, during the fifteen years prior to the era of Absolutism which is coming. Fouquet the prodigy, confident and blind, not having been able to comprehend the Queen Mother, nor retain Mazarin, nor evaluate the scheming Colbert, nor foresee Louis the Great, who condemned him for life, then stripped him of his splendor.

Appendix 3

Notes on the Fouquet Family

François and Marie Fouquet: "Their faith could be traced in their practical charity." One of the more striking of the seventeenth-century churches that line the rue Sainte-Antoine is Paris is Sainte-Marie-des-Anges, with its massive but elegant dome that provided a model for the dome of the Invalides. Built by the architect François Mansart for the nuns of the Visitation of Saint Mary, the church received much of its funding from Francois and Marie Fouquet, who engaged actively with the order.

The nuns of the Visitation called themselves *Visitandines*, because their mission was to visit the poor and the sick. Their patron was one of the great figures of the Counter-Reformation, Saint Vincent de Paul.

Madame Fouquet became in 1634 one of the "Ladies of Charity," a group of highborn women whom the priest assigned to aid the sick in Paris's most notorious hospital, the Hotel-Dieu.

> Working here demanded real commitment. In spite of the dangers to her own health—two Ladies of Charity died in the course of their duties—Marie made regular visits to the hospital, comforting the sick but also working hard to be of real practical assistance. She watched the patients carefully, noting the medicines that seemed

> to bring some genuine relief and those—by far the majority—which did not. She then went away and on the basis of her observation, concocted her own remedies. Soon she had developed a therapeutic skill that made her far more effective than the Augustinian nuns who were the official nurses in the hospital.[1]

The brother of Nicolas, Basile, with whom relations were often stormy, prepared a will shortly before his death in January of 1680—only months before Nicolas's. He had also, though an ecclesiastic, amassed a sizeable fortune. He too, like his brother, will go through a transformation in the final years before his passing. A biographer speaks of it more like the deep faith of the Fouquet family awakening in him. "Upon reading the document [his will], one confirms that the Christian, friend of the poor, *who sleeps inside of every Fouquet*, reappears. He takes the occasion to affirm the strong links that he preserves with the Visitation-Saint-Marie, *as with all the family*." In his last testament he bequeaths his goods to the surviving members of the Fouquet family and their manifold commitments to the life of Christian charity.[2]

Dessert writes about Nicolas at his final resting place. "Near to his father the Christian now reposes, at peace with his conscience, conformed to the pious and charitable example inherited from his parents."[3]

Mary Maupeou, the devout mother of Nicolas, will also be about the business of distributing her goods and making her final remarks as she feels death approaching. Dessert writes, "In concluding, the saintly woman thanks her children and grandchildren for their kindness, especially Mary Madeleine. She bequeaths to her two paintings of the Pietà kept in her room, with a chair, enclosing relics deposited at

[1] Charles Drazin, *The Man Who Outshone the Sun King: Ambition, Triumph and Treachery in the Reign of Louis XIV* (Random House, 2009), 9–10.

[2] Daniel Dessert, *Fouquet* (Fayard, 1987), 318 (emphasis added).

[3] Dessert, *Fouquet*, 288.

the Visitation-Sainte-Marie. She also pays a last and discreet homage to the superintendent, 'begging [Marie Madeleine] to thank her husband for the friendship he has always shown her, when it will have pleased God to bring them together, if she does not have the consolation of seeing them herself.'"[4]

Marie François Fouquet (1590–1681) was a French medical writer and philanthropist, child of Gilles de Maupeou and married to François IV Fouquet (1587–1640). She managed the hospital Dame de la Charité de l'Hôtel-Dieu in Paris (1634) and also served as director of l'Hôpital des Filles de la Providence in Paris (1658) and manager of the l'Hôpital des Dames de la Propagation de La Foi (1664).

A medical work that she wrote in 1685, the book *Les remèdes charitables de Madame Fouquet, pour guérir à peu de frais toute forme de maux tant internes qu'externes, invéterez, et qui ont passé jusques à présent pour incurables, experimentez par la même dame: et augmentez de la méthode que l'on pratique à l'Hôtel des Invalides pour guérir les soldats de la vérole* (The charitable remedies of Madame Fouquet, to cure at little cost all forms of evil, both internal and external, inveterate, and which have until now been considered incurable, used experimentally by the same lady: and augmenting the method that we practice at the Hôtel des Invalides to cure soldiers of smallpox), described her own experiments and treatments for various illnesses such as syphilis.

One of the craters of Venus bears her name.[5]

[4] Dessert, *Fouquet*, 320.

[5] See the Wikipedia entry for "Marie Fouquet," available online at https://en.wikipedia.org/wiki/Marie_Fouquet.

Acknowledgments

Several people gave of their time to offer counsel and assist with the research for this project. The former Head of the French Department at Vanderbilt (who also supervised my wife's PhD thesis), Virginia Scott, spoke with me by phone on the parameters of this project in its initial phases. Her younger colleagues at Vanderbilt responded to some arcane questions I was pursuing, chiefly around the identity of Michel Boutauld S.J. and questions about the conveyance of Fouquet's body to Paris.

Professor Stuart Weeks of Durham University was kind to forward me the bibliographic reference for his detailed archiving of works on Fouquet from the period in which *Les Conseils* was written.

Alexandre and Jean-Charles Vogüé, owners of Vaux-le-Vicomte, were friends of my late wife and on occasion have given clients from French Affaires a personal introduction to the chateau. Without our visits to Vaux, this book would never have been conceived.

My friend and colleague from the Jesuit Seminary in Paris, Brigitte Picq, was kind enough to respond to emails and forward questions to her colleagues there about the seventeenth-century literature associated with Boutauld and the genre of anonymous publication in this period.

Patrick Goujon S.J., Professor of Theology and the History of Spirituality at Facultés Loyola Paris, clarified some of the mysteries of Jesuit bibliography and cultural details relevant to seventeenth-century France. His notes are in appendix 1 prepared above.

I am grateful as well for the insightful responses of Professor Mark Elliot, my colleague at St Andrews and at Toronto. He is the kind of relentless master of the history of ideas one covets on any faculty.

The business my wife founded is now mine, and I am frequently in France, where my associate Maud Hacker lives. The walk down rue St Antoine in Paris is familiar to me, and now so too is the famous chapel where members of the Fouquet family rest.

The author of *The Man Who Outshone the Sun King*, Charles Drazin, though busy with another project at the time, reentered the world of his former research to respond to observations I was tendering about *Les Conseils*, a topic not discussed in his biography of Fouquet and about which he kindly showed interest. The final chapters of his book are sensitive to the spiritual transformation Fouquet was undergoing, and his work helped point me to the relevant French histories I needed to fill out the picture. Finally, there are friends in my present context who were kind enough to read drafts of the book, Sheila Butler and Karen Kutsko in particular. The world of seventeenth-century France takes some time to adjust to, and not every person has that kind of curiosity. Fortunately, the story of Fouquet, and of Ecclesiastes, makes for compelling reading.

With my late wife's death I lost a companion on a very unique journey, and I have sought to maintain trails we shared. A friend from our village observed that three areas of interest are still alive in my life: the spiritual and pastoral; the academic and authorial; and France. This book has allowed me to bring all three together. I am grateful to Baylor University Press and Dave Nelson for agreeing to publish what I hope will bring these three areas together for the reader as well, and to Cade Jarrell, Elyxandra Encarnación, Jenny Hunt, and Josh Mobley for production and marketing support.

Bibliography

Barbour, Jenni. *The Story of Israel in the Book of Qoheleth: Ecclesiastes as Cultural Memory*. Oxford University Press, 2012.

Boutauld, Michel. *Les conseils de la sagesse, ou le recueïl des maximes de Salomon les plus necessaires à l'homme pour se conduire sagement, avec des réflexions sur ces maximes*. Mabre-Cramoisy, 1677.

Boutauld, Michel. *The Counsels of Wisdom, or, A Collection of such Maxims of Solomon as are Most Necessary for the prudent Conduct of Life: With Proper Reflections upon them. Written Originally in French by Monseigneur Fouquet, Sometime Lord High Treasurer of France, in the Reign of Lewis XIV.* Done into English by [trans.] a Gent. With some Account of the Illustrious Author [identified as Fouquet]. Oxford, 1736.

Boutauld, Michel. *Méthode pour converser avec Dieu*. 13th ed. Bassompiere; Van den Berghen, 1770.

Boutauld, Michel. *Méthode pour converser avec Dieu*. Réédition au XIXème siècle. [1689] Ch. Amat, 1899.

Bundvad, Mette. *Time in the Book of Ecclesiastes*. Oxford University Press, 2015.

Chatelain, Urbain-Victor. *Le Surintendant Nicolas Foucquet, protecteur des lettres des arts et des sciences*. Perrin, 1905.

Chéruel, Adolphe. *Mémoires sur la vie publique et privée de Fouquet, Surintendant des Finances*. 2 vols. Charpentier, 1862.

Childs, Brevard S. *Exodus*. OTL. Westminster, 1974.

Childs, Brevard S. *Introduction to the Old Testament as Scripture*. Westminster, 1979.

Childs, Brevard S. "The *Sensus Literalis* of Scripture: An Ancient and Modern Problem." Pages 80–93 in *Beiträge zur alttestamentlichen Theologie: Festschrift für Walther Zimmerli zum 70. Geburtstag.* Edited by Herbert Donner, Robert Hanhart, and Rudolph Smend. Vandenhoeck & Ruprecht, 1977.

Childs, Brevard S. *The Struggle to Understand Isaiah as Christian Scripture.* Eerdmans, 2014.

Christianson, Eric. *Ecclesiastes Through the Centuries.* Blackwell Bible Commentaries. Wiley-Blackwell, 2008.

Christianson, Eric. *A Time to Tell: Narrative Strategies in Ecclesiastes.* Sheffield Academic, 1998.

Couton, Marie, Jérémie Christian, Isabelle Fernades, and Monique Vénuat, eds. *Emprunt plagiat, réécriture aux XVe, XVIe, XVIIe siècles: Pour un nouvel éclairage sur la pratique des lettres à la Renaissance.* Presses Universitaires Blaise-Pascal, 2006.

Dessert, Daniel. *Fouquet.* Fayard, 1987.

Drazin, Charles. *The Man Who Outshone the Sun King: Ambition, Triumph and Treachery in the Reign of Louis XIV.* Random House, 2009.

Dumas, Alexandre. *The Man in the Iron Mask.* Edited by David Coward. [1847] Oxford University Press, 1991.

Dumas, Alexandre. *The Vicomte de Bragelonne.* Edited by David Coward. [1850] Oxford University Press, 1995.

Giono, Jean. *Jean le Bleu.* Éditions Bernard Grasset, 1932. *Blue Boy.* Translated by Katherine A. Clark. Viking Press, 1946.

Fox, Michael V. "Aging and Death in Qoheleth 12." *JSOT* 42 (1988): 55–77.

Fox, Michael V. *Ecclesiastes: The Traditional Hebrew Text with the New JPS Translation.* JPS Bible Commentary. Jewish Publication Society, 2004.

Fox, Michael V. "Frame Narrative and Composition in the Book of Qoheleth." *HUCA* 48 (1977): 83–106.

Fox, Michael V. *A Time to Tear Down and a Time to Build Up: A Rereading of Ecclesiastes.* Eerdmans, 1999.

Johnston, Robert K. "Confessions of a Workaholic: A Reappraisal of Qoheleth." *CBQ* 38 (1976): 14–28.

Kynes, Will. *An Obituary for "Wisdom Literature": The Birth, Death, and Intertextual Reintegration of a Biblical Corpus.* Oxford University Press, 2019.

Kynes, Will. "Wisdom Literature: An Obituary." *JTS* 69 (2018): 1–24.

Lee, Eunny P. *The Vitality of Enjoyment in Qoheleth's Theological Rhetoric.* BZAW 353. de Gruyter, 2005.

Longman, Tremper. *The Book of Ecclesiastes.* NICOT. Eerdmans, 1998.

Morand, Paul. *Fouquet, ou le soleil offusqué.* Gallimard, 1961.

Petitfils, Jean-Christian. *Fouquet.* Perrin, 1998.

Seitz, Christopher R. "Booked Up: Ending John and Ending Jesus." Pages 91–102 in *Figured Out: Typology and Providence in Christian Scripture.* Westminster John Knox, 2001.

Seitz, Christopher R. "The Canonical Function of the *Nebi'im.*" Pages 167–81 in *Canon Formation: Tracing the Role of Sub-Collections in the Biblical Canon.* Edited by W. Edward Glenny and Darien R. Lockett. T&T Clark, 2023.

Seitz, Christopher R. "A Canonical Reading of Ecclesiastes." In *Acts of Interpretation: Scripture, Theology, and Culture.* Edited by S. A. Cummins and Jens Zimmerman. Eerdmans, 2018.

Seitz, Christopher R. *Convergences: Canon and Catholicity.* Baylor University Press, 2020.

Seitz, Christopher R. *Elder Testament: Canon, Theology, Trinity.* Baylor University Press, 2018.

Seitz, Christopher R. *The Heights of the Hills Are His Also.* Baylor University Press, 2024.

Seitz, Christopher R. "Job: Full Structure, Movement, and Interpretation." *Interpretation* 43 (1989): 5–17.

Sommervogel, Carlos. *Bibliothéque de la Compagnie de Jesus.* Nouvelle ed. Picard, 1841.

Verheij, Arian. "Paradise Retried: On Qoheleth 2:4–6." *JSOT* 50 (1991): 113–15.

Voltaire. *Le Siècle de Louis XIV.* Berlin, 1751.

Weeks, Stuart. *The Making of Many Books: Printed Works on Ecclesiastes 1523–1875.* Eisenbrauns, 2014.

Weeks, Stuart. "Solomon and Qoheleth." Pages 71–86 in *Megilloth Studies: The Shape of Contemporary Scholarship.* Edited by Brad Embry. Hebrew Bible Monographs 78. Sheffield Phoenix, 2016.

Whybray, Norman R. "Qoheleth, Preacher of Joy." *JSOT* 23 (1982): 87–98.

Wilkinson, Josephine. *The Man in the Iron Mask: The Truth About Europe's Most Famous Prisoner.* Pegasus Books, 2021.

Wilson, Gerald H. "'The Words of the Wise': The Intent and Significance of Qoheleth 12:9–14." *JBL* 103, no. 2 (1984): 175–92.

Wright, Addison G. "The Riddle of the Sphinx: The Structure of the Book of Qoheleth." *CBQ* 30 (1968): 313–34.

Wright, Addison G. "The Riddle of the Sphinx Revisited: Numerical Patterns in Qoheleth." *CBQ* 45 (1983): 32–43.

Wright, J. Robert, ed. *Proverbs, Ecclesiastes, Song of Solomon.* ACCS 9. IVP Academic, 2005.